HERTFORDSH
HEADLINES

★

HERTFORDSHIRE
HEADLINES

★

RICHARD WHITMORE

COUNTRYSIDE BOOKS
NEWBURY BERKSHIRE

Some of the material in this book was contained
in the book *Of Uncommon Interest,* published by
Spurbooks Ltd in 1975.

ISBN 0 905392 95 7
Produced through MRM (Print Consultants) Ltd., Reading
Typeset by SOS Typesetting, Reading
Printed in England by Borcombe Printers, Romsey

Contents

An Edwardian film cameraman. Outside the studio of Alpha Cinematograph Films, St Albans, in 1908, Arthur Melbourne-Cooper's brother Hubert showing off their hand-cranked moving picture camera. *(See The Film Pioneer of St Albans)*

Introduction

Nearly all the events recorded in this book made national – and in some cases international – news in Victorian and Edwardian times. Scandals, disasters, tragedies and acts of heroism which, for a short while, focused the nation's eyes upon my home county of Hertfordshire. I began collecting these stories about 15 years ago, when I was compiling my first book, *Of Uncommon Interest*. This has now been out of print for ten years and it was after enquiries from a new generation of local history enthusiasts about a possible reprint that I set about planning a revised edition called *Hertfordshire Headlines*. Having spent my working life chasing after the big headline news stories, it will come as no surprise to learn that I've selected for re-printing only the more sensational of those that appeared in *Of Uncommon Interest* and have added some new ones for good measure. As with my first book I have written the stories to try to give a flavour of the attitudes which existed among the ordinary people of that time and to show how they reacted to those events which affected their lives with particular force.

What, I hope, makes the stories more interesting is the fact that some are illustrated for the first time with contemporary photographs; for, although the plate camera was widely used throughout the last half of the 19th century it was not until the early 1900s that newspapers developed the first screen block-making machines that enabled them to reproduce photographs on newsprint. In the days prior to that stories could be illustrated only with the help of rather crude woodcut blocks such as the drawing of the poisoner Mary Ansell. So, the only real chance a photographer had of making any money from his 'scoop' was by working through the night with his assistant to produce hundreds of postcard prints which were then offered for sale to the public the following morning. The more sensational the story – the more he sold. For instance, during the three days after the great fire of Gaddesden Place, the Hemel Hempstead photographer P.T. Culverhouse, sold more than 3,000 postcard pictures of the burnt-out mansion. Indeed, I would like to think that this book is as much a tribute to the work of the early news

7

photographers as it is to the journalists of that period upon whose information I have relied so much during my researches.

It is also worth recalling the difficult conditions these men worked under. No comfortable cars to get them to the scene; no lightweight motorised cameras; no fast film nor synchronised flashlight equipment for them! Some had a pony and trap but many covered their assignments either on foot or on a bicycle, setting off (with an assistant if they were lucky) on a ten-mile journey, weighed down by the heavy wooden plate camera and tripod strapped to their backs and carrying cumbersome wooden cases which contained the large glass plates upon which they made their exposures. There were a good many such men in Hertfordshire, probably two or three in each main town by the 1870s, which makes it all the more irritating that such a small portion of their prolific output has survived to be appreciated today. On the other hand, their very scarcity makes the discovery of long-forgotten prints all the more exciting.

My own first encounter with Victorian news items occurred within a week of beginning my journalistic career in the early 1950s. As a junior reporter on the *Hertfordshire and Bedfordshire Express* I was assigned to the weekly task of climbing into a dusty loft above the editor's office, shooing out the pigeons and retrieving one of the dozens of bound and battered volumes of yesteryear that were stored there. From the brittle pages I had to select and type out a short item of about 100 words which I considered gave an interesting and contrasting view of life in Hitchin and district *'75 Years Ago'* as the little feature was called. It was a job which must have rated very low on the newspaper's productivity charts, mainly because I used to let it take up nearly the whole of one morning. This was not because I had difficulty finding an item; rather that I found too many, being lured from page to page by fascinating accounts of runaway cattle in the High Street, by amazing advertisements for *Dr William's Pink Pills for Pale People* (which apparently cured everything from gallstones to anaemia) and by such macabre stories as the one about the publican who caused an uproar in the town when he tried to boost trade one day by laying out for public view in his bar the corpses of a young couple killed in a road accident!

8

Not surprisingly, while assembling this series of stories, I have found myself wondering how they would have been treated in the Television Age. There's little doubt that, because of its insatiable daily demand for new information and fresh topics of discussion, the medium would have seized upon all of them. Cameramen and reporters would have been at Watford in plenty of time to record the astonishing street battles and looting the night they cancelled King Edward VII's coronation celebrations; imagine, too, the heated studio debates that would have followed the disclosure that the train disaster at Royston was caused by a quarter of a mile of faulty track which had rotted away through neglect. And what an outcry there would have been from the conservationists about the arrival in our country lanes of the motor car – particularly the one involved in a fatal collision at 20 miles per hour which resulted in the chauffeur being prosecuted for 'manslaughter by furious driving.' The two sensational murders of 1899 and the rows over capital punishment and police apathy that followed them would undoubtedly have filled a lot of air time as well.

No – attitudes and lifestyles may have changed over the past 100 years but, when it comes to the need to be thrilled or shocked by a headline of red hot news, the public's appetite remains as strong now as ever it was in Victoria's day.

Richard Whitmore
Hitchin
Hertfordshire   1987

Acknowledgements

The author is indebted to the following organisations for providing help and facilities during his researches: The British Museum Newspaper Library, Colindale; Hertfordshire County Record Office; The Hertfordshire Local Studies Collection; Hertfordshire Fire Brigade; Hertfordshire Constabulary; John Dickinson's Paper Mills, Hemel Hempstead; Hitchin Museum; Stevenage Museum; Watford Reference Library; Ashwell Museum; Hertford Museum; The Historical Records Department of British Rail and Syndication International Ltd. London.

The following publications were used for reference; *A History of The British Fire Service* by Geoffrey Blackstone; *A Venture of Faith* by Miss E A Latchmore; *The Story of Hertfordshire Police* by Neil Osborn; *Family Notes and Reminiscences* by Sir Kenneth Murchison; *Hitchin Worthies* by Reginald Hine; *Zeppelin!* by Raymond Laurence Rimell and *Fire over England* by H G Castle. *The Daily Mail, The Daily Mirror, The Times, The North Herts Gazette Series (The Hertfordshire & Bedfordshire Express), The Hertfordshire Mercury, The Herts Advertiser, The Watford Observer, The Barnet Press, The Royston Crow, The Luton News* and *The Hemel Hempstead Gazette*.

The author also thanks all the individuals who have given him valuable help during the writing of *Hertfordshire Headlines* – particularly Ron Warner of Cuffley, for access to his collection of airship photographs; to Beryl Carrington of St Albans for background to the story of Mary Ansell; to Jan Wadowski, also of St Albans, son-in-law of the city's film pioneer, Arthur Melbourne-Cooper, for the loan of photographs; to Geoffrey Harris of Letchworth for the photograph of the Watford rioters.

Conflagration!

★

Gaddesden Place, near Hemel Hempstead, went up in flames during the early hours of 1st February, 1905. The events which form the climax to this chapter were not chosen simply for reasons of sensationalism. They also illustrate the enormous problems which could confront the small and ill-equipped fire brigades upon whom most of the country relied at the turn of the century. The two main brigades which had to cope with the incident were typical of hundreds in existence at that time – one a private brigade of paid firemen, the other a group of 'gentlemen volunteers'. Their equipment, which had changed very little during the last half of the 19th century, consisted of horse-drawn pumps, operated by hand, hoses of leather or poor quality canvas and (their only effective mechanised aid) a coal-fired steamer to pump water to the scene.

The Hemel Hempstead Volunteer Fire Brigade was formed in 1845 after a town meeting, called with some urgency to discuss ways of coping with 'the spirit of incendiarism' which had made its appearance in the area. At this time, fire-raising was very common, a popular but cowardly form of revenge by disgruntled or ill-treated workers against their employers and a convenient way of delaying the progress of mechanisation which, many of the poorer classes believed, was destined to put them out of work. In 1831, for example, more than nine hundred men were convicted of setting fire to the new and hated threshing machines which were causing unemployment on the farms. This, in spite of the fact that arson was still a crime which carried the ultimate penalty. In December 1833, John Stallan of Shelford in Cambridgeshire achieved the unenviable distinction of becoming the last man in Britain to be executed for fire-raising. He confessed to starting ten fires in his village, not for the usual motive of revenge, but because he was a volunteer fireman who enjoyed

11

his work and felt he wasn't getting enough of it! He told the judge at Cambridge Assizes that he did it for the free beer and money that went with the work.

Against this sort of background, then, the citizens of Hemel Hempstead organised their first volunteer fire-fighting force to back up the work of the only other small brigade in the district which was financed and run by an insurance company. The minutes of that inaugural meeting in 1845 recorded that the volunteer brigade should consist of certain *gentlemen,* who would provide uniforms and hats at their own expense, and certain *men* who would be paid for their work and would receive uniforms free of charge. In addition a number of 'pioneers' were appointed; their duty was to gallop ahead of the brigades during an alarm to locate water supplies close to the scene of the fire. These two brigades served the community until the 1880s, when the insurance company brigade was disbanded to be replaced shortly afterwards by a new one, belonging to the giant John Dickinson Paper Mills. This private brigade, formed in 1883, was the second one to feature strongly in the disaster at Gaddesden Place. It was the Dickinson brigade, too, which possessed the much envied steamer.

The steam fire engine was the most important development in fire-fighting equipment during the Victorian era. It has been invented as far back as 1829 by John Braithwaite and had put up an impressive performance at its first fire in London a year later, sending jets of water ninety feet high, into the blazing Argyll Rooms on a bitterly cold February night which had frozen all the manual pumps solid. Yet it was never adopted by any of the big city brigades; for some strange reason the chief fire officers regarded it with suspicion, some declaring it too powerful to do a proper job! Braithwaite's steamer was also much disliked by the volunteers working the manual pumps and, on several occasions when Braithwaite turned up at a big fire with his machine, the pumpers, to ensure they were going to continue in work, slashed the hoses! It was not until thirty years later that brigades finally came to acknowledge the value of the steamer which, by this time, was being produced by two London companies, Shand Mason, and Merryweathers. In 1878, Merryweathers were adver-

The earliest-known photograph of a British fire brigade. Hemel Hempstead Volunteers in 1845, the year of their formation 'to cope with the spirit of incendiarism.' Hoses, helmets and buckets are of leather.

tising that they had sold more than five hundred steamers to brigades up and down the country, but it was only the wealthier, private brigades such as Dickinsons, and those in the big cities, which could afford them. Dickinsons bought theirs in 1893 for £340.

It was a momentous day when a town took delivery of the first steamer. Often its arrival at the railway station was greeted by a guard of honour formed by the local firemen and other brigades from neighbouring towns. Preceded by a brass band they would pull the steamer proudly through the town to the fire station where a group of civic dignitaries would be waiting, among them some prominent local lady who had been invited to 'christen' the machine by breaking a bottle of champagne over the footplate. The names given to these steamers were often exotic; *Firefly*, *Ajax* and *Torrent*. Some were christened *Prince Albert*, or *The Victoria*, the name being painted boldly in gold lettering on the side of the machine. Later, those steamers which developed any irritating faults or peculiarities while functioning

13

at fires would be given rather less flattering names by their operators; *Puffing Polly, Belching Bertha,* or as on one occasion *Farting Annie.* Nevertheless, whatever abuse the firemen may have heaped on their machines during the stresses of fire-fighting they were tremendously proud of them, and many brigades changed their titles from the Volunteer Fire Brigade to the Volunteer *Steam* Fire Brigade, in order to distinguish themselves from their less well-off neighbours who were still working with the old manual pumps.

The turnout of the local horse-drawn steamer was an event which never failed to thrill children and adults alike. For the firemen, though, it was a carefully rehearsed procedure which varied from station to station depending on the size of the town. In rural areas, the brigade often had to rely not only on volunteer firemen but on volunteer horses as well, which meant that when the alarm bell sounded, the turnout of the steamer was always preceded by a hell-for-leather race between the butcher, the baker, the farmer and undertaker, each man galloping his horse to the fire station in an endeavour to be among the first two or three needed to make up the team and so claim the quite substantial fee which the brigade paid for the service. Other brigades preferred to have a regular contract with a local livery stable to supply horses specially trained for the job. With time, many of these animals came to recognise the significance of the sound of the alarm bell and would get very excited, anticipating the gallop and work that lay ahead. During the latter part of the last century, a liveryman at Ware who held the contract to provide a pair of horses for the town's brigade, had only to open his stable doors when the bell sounded, and the horses would canter smartly round to the fire station unaccompanied! In the bigger cities, the firemen kept their own beasts, spending hours training them to respond to the bell by trotting out of their stable to a point beneath their specially designed harness which was suspended from the ceiling by pulleys, so it could be quickly lowered on to the animals' backs. Each harness had an unusual split collar which dropped over the horse's neck and was clipped together underneath. Features such as this in the design of the equipment enabled many brigades to turn out in less than two minutes.

14

The steamer itself was kept with a small gas jet burning permanently beneath the boiler, so that the water in it was kept just short of steam pressure. The fire beneath the boiler was, of course, laid ready, coal at the bottom, then sticks and finally paper on top. While the coachman and firemen were busy harnessing the horses, it was the engineer's job to run to his steps at the back of the steamer and throw a special long-burning fuse match down the funnel. The draught which resulted during the hair-raising ride was always sufficient to ensure that the boiler fire was burning well by the time the steamer arrived at the scene. Few Victorians or Edwardians ever forgot the sight of a steamer on its way to a blaze. The coachman yelling encouragement to his horses and handling them with magnificent precision along the narrow and often congested streets, the officer in charge along-side him ringing the bell and operating the handbrake where necessary, the firemen crouched in two lines along the hose box, and the engineer, clinging precariously to his handgrips, on the footplate at the rear.

By the 1870s the Fire Brigade Competitions had got into full swing and were being organised on a national scale. The principal manufacturers of the engines, Shand Mason and Merryweathers, were offering generous prizes to the winners. On such 'friendly' contest was held at Watford in 1877 which, while providing great excitement for the huge crowd, also degenerated into a slanging match between the losers and the judges. This stemmed from the fact that most of the volunteer brigades were still very much a law unto themselves, with little regard for any national code of fire-fighting procedures which may have existed, and each quite convinced and their ideas about drill and fire-fighting techniques were the right ones. Engineer Penfold, of the Metropolitan Fire Brigade, who had the misfortune to be one of the judges at this event, returned dazed to London to pen the following report to his seniors:

'I would respectfully beg that I am strongly of the opinion that these volunteer contests should find judges from their own class, as each competing brigade will always persist in following their own particular ideas, instead of following rules laid down, and will insist that their own peculiar ways are correct, and that all others are wrong and – as trickery is a great element in nearly all of them – it makes the office of judge for an impartial man a very unsatisfactory office.'

If the volunteer firemen of Victorian Hertfordshire were an arrogant race, that arrogance was merely a reflection of extreme pride in their unit. Most were tough extroverts, a dedicated élite who, usually for no money at all, were prepared to take enormous risks in what they regarded as the normal course of duty. Some brigades, in fact, charged a subscription, so that the 'gentlemen volunteers' actually paid for the privilege of putting out the town's fires. Because many local authorities were slow to recognise their worth, brigades also had to rely on voluntary contributions and fund-raising events to buy their equipment. An episode at St Albans in 1899 illustrates just how much a brigade could be taken for granted and how quick the public were to criticise, when on just one occasion things went wrong.

During the evening when a fire broke out in a photographic studio in Alma Road, most members of the volunteer brigade were, it seems, scattered about various public houses in the town which, not unnaturally, were not connected to the alarm bell system. As a result the brigade was slow to turn out – very slow. According to most estimates it was something like forty-five minutes before the engine arrived at the scene, even though the street where the fire was burning was only a five-minute walk from the fire station. By this time, the studio was virtually destroyed. The incident caused an uproar which filled many columns of the local newspaper for weeks to come and set the City Council thinking seriously about whether the brigade should be taken over by the Police. The brigade captain at that time was a local ironmonger and engineer, Captain William Thorpe, who, far from being deterred by the criticism seized upon it to bring home to the citizens of St Albans the great difficulties under which their brigade was working. He pointed out that they had only been able to purchase their Merryweather steamer a few years earlier by launching an appeal.

'No one can foresee the future, no one can do impossibilities,' he wrote. 'Fires do not break out by appointment and if, as unfortunately happened in the recent case, a fire occurs at an

16

hour when men are leaving work and seeking an hour's recreation away from home and consequently cannot be communicated with – either at their homes or place of work – delay in their arrival at the scene of the outbreak is, of necessity, bound to arise.'

The incident served to jerk the City Council out of its distant critical attitude; they met the firemen and together threshed out a scheme for improvements. A site for a new fire station was found and a resident caretaker employed to act as coachman for the fire engine. In 1901 the council resolved to pay the volunteers for their services. They would in future receive 2s. 0d. for the first hour's work at a fire and 1s. 6d. an hour thereafter. 'St Albans,' said one city alderman, 'has a very efficient brigade and it is not fair that they should be called upon to put their hands in their own pockets to defray the expenses of their work.'

That same year, 1901, the John Dickinson Fire Brigade achieved what must then have been the goal of every dedicated fire team in the country; at the National Fire Brigades' Union camp at Basingstoke they became national champions, winning the National Steamer Drill Final in what was then an impressive record time of 35.2 seconds. In the exercise, working with a strange engine and horses, they had to make a flying start, gallop the team fifty yards, unhook the horses, connect up three fifty feet lengths of hose and hit a target with their jet. After the Duke of Marlborough had presented them with their trophy, they were invited to repeat the demonstration. They accepted, and astonished the crowd by knocking a further three seconds off the record time which they had clocked up earlier in the afternoon.

By the turn of the century the Fire Brigades' Union had done much to establish a national code of standards for firemen and this had helped to remove the undignified squabbles and scenes which had accompanied earlier competitions. There was, nevertheless, still considerable rivalry between neighbouring brigades and it was not unknown for a fire to rage merrily on while the captains of the various brigades indulged in heated argument over who was to take control of the operation. It was to remove what one officer called 'these petty jealousies' that the two brigades at Hemel Hempstead, Dickinsons and the Volunteer Brigade, began to train together, organising combined drills,

'The flames had the mastery....' P.T. Culverhouse's re-touched night photo-graph of Gaddesden Place as the fire engulfed the main block.

which in the event of a major fire would enable them to pool their resources in the most effective way possible. Their first chance to put the results of those combined drills to the test came on the night Gaddesden Place went up in flames.

The mansion, which stood on a hill three miles to the north-west of Hemel Hempstead, was built in 1774 by the Halsey family, who had owned the estate for many generations. The current owner was the Right Honourable Thomas Halsey, Member of Parliament for West Hertfordshire who, at that time, was living with his family at their London home and had rented Gaddesden Place to a fellow parliamentarian, the M.P. for Preston, John Kerr. It was he, his wife and daughters, and a large corps of servants, who were in residence on the night of the fire. In retros-pect, it was a fire that should never have happened. For several days the family and staff had been concerned about the strong smell of burning throughout the house, and on Tuesday 31st

18

January, it had become so strong that the estate carpenter and other workmen were called in to try to discover the source. They examined the large boiler in the cellar and the heating pipes, but could find nothing wrong. Nobody considered it worthwhile to call in the fire brigade for advice; had they done so the brigade would almost certainly have discovered the smouldering beam near a boiler flue-pipe, which had been burning for days and which finally broke loose into a room in the main block of the house at 4 a.m. on 1st February.

The alarm was raised by one of the Kerr daughters and within five minutes the whole household had been alerted and evacuated outside, still in their nightclothes. One of the estate workers saddled a horse and galloped the three miles into Hemel Hempstead to sound the fire alarm. At 4.23 a.m. the brigade's horse-drawn manual pump, with Captain Harry Hancock in charge, was on its way. 'Telephonic messages' were despatched to the John Dickinson brigade at 4.40 a.m. and they arrived at 5.30 a.m. with Second Officer James Burles in charge. By this time, the main block of the house was well alight. Estate workers had formed a human chain and were desperately trying to save the valuable contents of Thomas Halsey's library, his paintings, antique furniture and numerous other priceless heirlooms, but a strong wind was blowing and they had saved only a small proportion of the contents before the flames surged through the corridors and engulfed every room in the main block.

It was a hopeless task for the firemen; their only real chance was to try to contain the fire in the main block and save the two wings which housed the servants' quarters and the laundry. They might have done more if they had had a supply of water nearby but, apart from a small domestic supply, the nearest was half a mile away in the River Gade at the bottom of the hill. Hancock and Burles put their heads together and decided to send the Dickinson steamer down to the river to pump water up the hill to a dam, from which the manual pumps could then draw their water. To achieve this, the firemen laid and connected 1,800 feet of hose between the steamer by the river, and the house. The steamer worked perfectly but the incline leading to the house was too great, and when the water pressure reached 120lb, the

19

canvas hoses burst. The only other source of water was from a pond on a neighbouring estate some 2,500 feet away across a small valley. To get this water across to the house was a mammoth task using just about every inch of hose that the four brigades now on the scene could supply. Incredibly, they did it. The Dickinson steamer at the pond and then the three manual pumps from Hemel Hempstead, Frogmore and Berkhamsted stretched across Gaddesden Park in a relay, pumping the water from one team to the next until it reached the hoses trained on the burning mansion. With great difficulty they managed to provide an erratic supply which was at least sufficient to enable the firemen to save the two wings of the building.

The reporter from the *Hemel Hempstead Gazette* who witnessed the event wrote: 'The flames had the mastery and leapt higher and higher and issued from windows on all sides of the mansion. As the dense volumes of smoke continued to rise, and as crash after crash of windows smashing, ceilings and floors falling through, walls cracking and masonry-work tumbling, the sight was appalling and terrible to behold. The firemen battled with the flames until they were beaten back time and time again and, the high wind blowing right to the inside of the building, every room of the main block became enveloped. It was noticed that the lead covering the coping was running down the walls, so intense was the heat.'

During the desperate struggle to get water to the scene there were several angry exchanges between the firemen and the volunteers working the manual pumps. James Burles, officer in charge of the Dickinson brigade, referred in his report to 'the disgraceful behaviour of the pumpers, bringing discredit to the various brigades', by failing to keep up a steady supply of water. Finding men to work the pumps was obviously more difficult in a remote country area like Gaddesden, than in a town where there were always plenty of volunteers eager for the 1s. 0d. an hour normally paid to the pumpers. It was exhausting work, the teams rarely able to work efficiently for more than five minutes at a stretch. Twenty-four men were needed to operate each pump (twelve on each side) with a second team of the same number standing by to relieve them. On this occasion there were not enough men to

20

make up a relief team which meant that on several occasions during critical periods when the fire was at its height, the pumpers collapsed from exhaustion and the supply of water to the hoses stopped.

The firemen had to work on the building throughout the whole of Wednesday dealing with sporadic outbreaks which threatened the wings of the burnt-out mansion, but by the evening the situation was considered well under control. Two of the brigades were stood down, leaving the Hemel Hempstead and Dickinson brigades on duty. Hundreds of sightseers had come and gone and even the firemen and estate workers were beginning to relax when, belatedly and at one horrifying stroke, the fire reached out and snatched two victims.

William Paton, aged 45, had been butler to the Kerr family for only a few days and had spent the previous twelve hours worrying about the safety of the large store of wine in the cellars beneath Gaddesden Place. At the height of the fire he had organised a chain of staff to remove most of the cases from the cellar to the safety of the garden. Later on, worried about the possiblity of looting after dusk, and when it seemed there was no danger of the fire reaching the cellar, he decided to have them replaced. He told his employer of his decision and Mr Kerr warned him: 'Don't take any unnecessary risks. Lose all the wine rather than a life.' Paton, however, went ahead and all the cases were returned to the cellar.

With all the wine replaced, the butler was standing in the vaults with four other men — his footman James Jones, aged 21, a fireman Sidney Clark, P.C. Limbrick and in elderly helper, Alfred Dolt. Suddenly, a beam in one of the main walls burst into flames. The butler turned to the fireman with a look of alarm on his face.

'What do you think of that lot?' he asked. 'Is it safe?'

Fireman Clark assured him that it was not, and so, for the second time, the butler decided to move all the wine out. He ordered Jones the footman to go for help to move the wine cases again, but before the young man could take a step there was a deafening crash.

Paton was heard to scream 'My God!' and the next moment was buried beneath several feet of red-hot bricks as one of the main walls of the building above them crashed through the cellar roof. When his body was eventually dug out of the rubble the next morning it was burned beyond recognition – the only consolation that could be offered by the surgeon who examined the corpse was that William Paton had died instantaneously, his neck broken by the weight of the falling masonry. James Jones, the footman, was not accorded such a merciful end. As the bricks cascaded into the cellar he was thrown, still upright, into a corner where he stood pinned up to his shoulders by the hot rubble. The other three, caught only by the extremities of the collapse, managed to stagger from the cellar for help. It was dark by this time but the rescuers, with a lantern and guided by the agonised cries of 'Help-me – I'm burning!' quickly located the young man in the thick dust and confusion of the cellar. Red-hot ashes were falling on his head, the only part of him that was visible above the bricks. While Captain Hancock played a hose on the rubble to try to cool it, others set to work with pick and shovel, ignoring the danger of a possible further collapse above them. It took them forty-five minutes to free the victim, James Jones remaining conscious throughout the ordeal and pleading with his rescuers to try to save the butler. The rescuers, however, knew that was pointless. The footman was eventually released and taken to hospital, but his burns were so severe that he was unable to survive the shock and died the following morning as the firemen returned to the mansion to begin their long search for the body of the butler.

The following week, after an inquest had recorded verdicts of 'accidental death' on the two victims, the volunteer firemen of Hemel Hempstead held an emergency meeting at the Swan Hotel. Captain Hancock made a forthright statement about shortcomings which the Gaddesden Place fire, the most serious in the history of their brigade, had brought to light. Unlike his opposite number in charge of the Dickinson brigade he did not level criticism at the pumpers who, he said, had worked until they could work no more. He blamed their out-of-date equipment and said the time had come when the people of Hemel Hempstead should seriously consider providing the town with a steam engine. The Town Council had been approached before about this and also about providing a new fire station but according to Captain Hancock, 'While promises have been made, nothing has been done.'

Hancock's remarks found their way home. Both the council and private individuals responded quickly and in the following year, 1906, the foundation stone was laid for a new fire station and a public appeal launched to buy the Hemel Hempstead brigade their first steamer. Although they were late in getting one, they were by no means the last, for the old horse-drawn steamer took a long time dying. The first self-propelled motor fire engines may have appeared, but they caught on very slowly indeed, particularly since some of them couldn't travel as fast as a well managed horse-drawn steamer! In addition, many brigades displayed an attitude similar to their predecessors in mid-Victorian times who had been convinced that steam pumps would never replace the old manuals. Mechanical transport, they believed, was a passing fad and the horse would never be dispensed with. Consequently, it was not until the First World War that the thrilling spectacle of the old horse-drawn steamer finally began to disappear from the towns and villages of Britain.

The Public Murder of Mercy Nicholls

★

It was 3.30 a.m. when the caller hammered on the front door of No 13 Railway Street, Hertford on a March night in 1899. Mr Frederick Davis, a musician, and his wife Elizabeth, in the upstairs front bedroom of their terraced house, lay for a moment wondering whether to go down and answer it. Their home was on the edge of a rough area, close to several pubs and lodging houses, and street rowdies had been a problem recently. Eventually, Mrs Davis got up, opened the bedroom window and leaned out to see who was there. The sky was overcast and it had been raining but there was sufficient light for her to make out the figure of a slightly-built young man with fair hair. He was looking up at her.

'Missus,' he called out. 'Will you lend me an axe?'

'An axe?' queried Mrs Davis. 'What do you want with an axe?'

'To chop this woman's head off,' he replied.

Mrs Davis pause for a moment to reassure herself that she was awake and that she had heard the chilling request correctly. Then, with some trepidation, she leaned a little further out of the window to look for the woman in question. There was no-one else in sight.

'What woman?' she asked.

'Just a minute,' said the young man and hurried off across the street to a hall belonging to the Young Men's Christian Association. He disappeared into the blackness of the doorway and emerged dragging the apparently lifeless and near-naked body of a woman. It was at this point that Mrs Davis decided to scream for help.

First to hear her were Henry Wright and his son Ebenezer who were passing the end of the street in a horsedrawn cart on their way to milk cows at a farm in Ware. They turned up the

24

The scene of Mercy Nicholl's murder, Railway Street, Hertford as it appeared in the late 1880s.

street and saw the young man who, by then, had started to drag the woman up and down Railway Street, pausing occasionally to stab at her with what appeared to be a pocket knife or else throwing her to the ground and kicking her. They had been watching this brutal scene for several minutes thinking the blood-stained woman was already dead when suddenly she began moaning 'Oh God! Help me! I am dying! Is there some water?' Whereupon her attacker shouted at her 'You shall not have any!' and commenced kicking her again.

At this point young Ebenezer Wright suddenly realised that he knew the man. 'That's Rotten Smith,' he whispered to his father. 'His real name's John Smith but we call him Rotten.' Instructing his 16-year-old son to stay and watch from a safe distance Mr Wright drove to Hertford Police Station, about a quarter of a mile away, to raise the alarm. He reached there at 3.40 a.m. and told P.C. Robert Sherman, who was on desk duty:

'There's a man killing a woman, if she's not already dead, against Mrs Davis's near Bull Plain. She's naked and her face is bleeding.' To Mr Wright's astonishment P.C. Sherman told him that he couldn't leave the station and there was nothing he could do until P.C. Langstone, whose beat covered Railway Street, called in in a few minutes time. In fact P.C. Langstone never showed up and for the next two hours the dying woman was dragged up and down Railway Street suffering further attacks from the madman.

At the Coroner's inquest later it was revealed that several other residents had heard the noise, opened their windows to see what was going on and hurriedly closed them again, not wishing to get involved. Charlie Papper, the corporation lamp-lighter, didn't wish to get involved either. Just after 4 a.m. he appeared on his rounds and found Smith doing a mock drill in the middle of the street, shouting 'Halt. Who goes there?' at the top of his voice. The woman was lying nearby in the gutter, still crying for help. 'She was stabbed all over the face and was unrecognisable; her clothing had been stripped from her,' Mr Papper told the inquest jury, confessing: 'I proceeded on my rounds as quickly as I could.' A juror: 'So you thought it more important to put out your lamps than help the woman?'
Charlie: 'Well, it confused me so and frightened me so that I didn't know what to do.'
Juror: 'Didn't it strike you to go to the Police Station?'
Charlie: 'No it didn't.'

However, between 5 o'clock and 5.30 at least three other citizens who also witnessed the attack *did* go to the police station and told P.C. Sherwood about it – but still nothing was done. No Policemen turned up and no residents challenged Smith nor tried to help the poor woman. At just after 6 o'clock, when a policeman finally appeared on the scene, John Smith had gone, leaving the woman lying in a pool of blood under an archway next to *The Diamond* public house. P.C. Daniel Hewitt found Smith's pocket knife lying nearby. The woman was still alive when the ambulance cart took her to Hertford General Hospital but, despite the efforts of the doctors, she died at 9.30 a.m.

Her name was Mercy Nicholls, from the neighbouring town

of Ware. She was 27 years old, and had been married six years to a man who worked in a local brickworks. They had recently separated and, while staying with her mother at Cole Green, Mercy Nicholls had met John Smith, then only 17, and had gone to stay with him in one of the lodging houses near Railway Street. Smith was described as 'a bit short on intellect but did not drink and was not normally a quarrelsome or violent man'. He had recently spent a year working for a local clergyman as a gardener/handyman and at the time that he met Mercy was waiting to join the Hertfordshire Militia.

As the story of this astonishing incident was pieced together it emerged that the couple had been out drinking the previous night and, although Smith appeared sober, Mercy Nicholls was very drunk and noisy. What happened to cause Smith's mind to snap was never discovered. Witnesses reported that they had seen the couple weaving their way along nearby streets shouting abuse at each other between midnight and 1 a.m. Mrs Jane Papper, wife of the lamplighter, told the inquest that she heard a woman screaming 'Oh God, I am dying,' as early as 2.25 a.m. but did nothing about it. When asked why not she replied: 'If we got up every time we heard a row in the street we would be getting up every minute.'

So it would appear that for at least four hours, probably longer, Smith dragged his victim up and down the street beating and multilating her until he abandoned her and returned to the lodging house where he cheerfully confessed to all and sundry that he had 'done for a woman' in Railway Street. With two other men, the proprietor of the lodging house took him round to the police station where he was detained. He subsequently appeared at the Summer Assizes where, after evidence from doctors at Herts County Lunatic Asylum, John 'Rotten' Smith was declared insane and therefore unfit to plead to the charge of murder. Mr Justice Mathew ordered that he be detained during Her Majesty's pleasure.

With the verdict a foregone conclusion, Press and Public were less interested in John Smith than they were in the astonishing behaviour of the residents of Railway Street and certain members of the county constabulary. Why had no-one gone to help the stricken woman, and why had the police failed to turn out for what was clearly a serious incident, taking place only a short distance from the police station? At the inquest, the residents – like lamplighter Charlie Papper – made no bones about it; they were scared. Young Ebenezer Wright, the cowman's son who had shown considerable courage by staying with Smith while his father went to report the matter, was asked whether he'd seen any policemen while he had waited there. 'No,' he replied 'We never do see a policeman in Hertford.'

The police fared very badly at the inquest. Questioned by the coroner, Mr T.J. Sworder, P.C. Robert Sherwood was asked whether he had any specific instructions on what to do if someone came in at night to report a serious incident. He said that if there were any cases of burglary, fire or murder, he was to call the Superintendent or Sergeant Gardner, both of whom were asleep in the police station in rooms connected to the front office by means of a speaking tube. The first time P.C. Sherwood used the tube was at 5.35 a.m. when the fourth or fifth witness reported the incident. Asked why he had not responded in that way two hours earlier, Sherwood said it did not seem serious.

And what of the mysterious P.C. Herbert Langstone who was supposed to be patrolling the Railway Street area that night but who never appeared? He claimed that he had returned to the police station at 3.30 a.m. and as there was no reports and he was wet, he had told P.C. Sherwood he would 'keep on walking' and continued patrolling another part of Hertford. He did not bother to return to the station and went home to bed when his tour of duty finished. He had been in Railway Street at 1.30 a.m. 'Everything was so quiet I did not trouble to come down again. When all is quiet I devote my time to other parts of the beat,' he said.

The Coroner: 'Langstone, I am sorry to say I do not believe you.'

The Chief Constable of Hertfordshire, Lt.Col Henry Daniell, had acted swiftly when news of his officers' scandalous behaviour got out and at the end of the long and painstaking inquest he told the coroner and jury that he had made a close examination of all the sergeants and officers on duty that night and had found that all were strictly and punctually on duty except Langstone.

28

'I do not believe Langstone's evidence either,' he said. 'I believe he was at home or lying up somewhere where he should not have been.' Returning a verdict of 'murder' the jury added a rider that 'we consider the conduct of PCs Sherwood and Langstone deserving of the greatest censure and their evidence is not to be relied upon. We exonerate the rest of the police from any blame.'

In fact, both Langstone and Sherwood had been dismissed from the force before the inquest but neither this nor the jury's exoneration of the force itself satisfied the community. Numerous letters had already appeared in the local and national newspapers expressing very strong feelings of unease at the fact that such an incident could happen. The *Hertfordshire Mercury* commented: 'The whole story is too revolting to dwell upon and casts a foul blot upon the fair name of this town.' An M.P. put down a question to the Home Secretary suggesting the facts should be placed before The Director of Public Prosecutions and that Sherwood and Langstone should be prosecuted for neglect of duty and cowardice. The Mayor of Hertford, Mr Hellier Gosselin, demanded that Hertfordshire's Police Authority, The Standing Joint Committee, should conduct a full inquiry into the affair – which they did.

Their report, published several weeks later, concluded that both policemen were very negligent in their duties and that it was probably not the first time that Langstone had failed to patrol properly, but they also criticised the force (and thereby The Chief Constable) for leaving too much to the constables themselves as to whether or not they patrolled their beats properly. So they ordered Col. Daniell to increase the supervision of beat constables at night, with senior officers carrying out far more snap checks. They also ordered that attendance books at police stations should be better-kept; that there should be more efficient patrolling of trouble spots like Railway Street and tighter controls on lodging houses. With a reputation for being a swift and positive decision-maker, the Chief Constable re-organised the beat system almost overnight.

Some years earlier, in 1880, Henry Daniell had been picked from 66 candidates to undertake the specific task of revitalising and reorganising Hertfordshire's flagging police force. When he

29

retired in 1911 he was credited with shaping 'one of the most efficient police forces in the whole kingdom.' The most serious challenge to that eminent career came in 1899 with the murder of Mercy Nicholls. For, as a doctor at the inquest pointed out, 'of the 59 wounds made by John Smith's pocket knife none was sufficiently serious to prove fatal. But with so many, Mercy Nicholls literally bled to death. If help had been afforded her when her cries were heard, the medical evidence shows that, in all probability, she would have recovered.'

The Markyate Motor Tragedies

★

For the hundreds of people who witnessed it, the scene in Fore Street, Hertford, one Thursday afternooon in May 1903 was unforgettable. The air throbbed with noise and was filled with exhaust fumes as the county town experienced its first traffic jam. The pioneer motorists were there at the invitation of the town mayor in what was a calculated public relations exercise to help apprehensive country folk understand and accept the generally unwelcome advent of the motor car.

The motoring mayor of Hertford, Mr Kenneth Murchison, had become one of the county's first car-owners two years earlier, when he paid 300 guineas for a 4½ horse-power de Dion-Bouton Voiturette.

Many years later, as Sir Kenneth Murchison, High Sheriff of Northamptonshire, he was to recall: 'It is quite impossible now for people to have any real conception of the experiences, pre-judices, hardships and insults which were suffered by the pioneers of motoring in this country... We were all outlaws together and we felt that the police and public opinion were against us. If there was an accident anywhere it must have been our fault, even if we were not there and knew nothing of it.'

In the year of 1901, shortly after acquiring his de Dion, Sir Kenneth was among the handful of Hertfordshire car owners who each received a peremptory circular from the Chief Constable of the county, Colonel Henry Daniell:

'The Chief Constable desires to inform owners and drivers of Motor Vehicles in the County of Hertford that constant com-plaints are made to him of the alarm and danger to the public caused by the reckless driving of some of these vehicles.

The Chief Constable reminds owners and drivers that the

31

One of Britain's first car rallies, held in Hertford in 1903.

speed at which a motor car may be driven on a highway is limited by law to TWELVE MILES AN HOUR. It by no means follows that this speed may be sustained when Motor Cars are passing or meeting other vehicles or horses, or when passing through towns, villages or other inhabited places. On each of these occasions it is incumbent on the drivers of Motor Cars to reduce their speed to such a pace as would be safe and reasonable were the vehicles drawn by horse instead of mechanical power. Failure to observe this precaution will render the driver of the Motor Car liable to prosecution under Article IV., Sec. I., of the Locomotives on Highways Act, 1896....'

The circular illustrates perfectly the fierce opposition which the early motorists met from a rural population still firmly convinced that the horse was the only respectable and reliable form of road transport. Unfortunately, it was the horses which were caused most distress by the presence of a car upon the road. Even when driven slowly, the noise of the engine and the dust it created were sufficient to make the most passive beast restive; the more volatile ones frequently became so terrified that they bolted, often throwing and injuring the rider.

Recalling from his diary the first time he took his wife for a ride in the de Dion, Sir Kenneth wrote: 'She sat in the front seat facing the way we were going, with nothing whatever between her feet resting on a board which folded forward for the purpose, and anything we might run into. We did run into several things that day – mostly animals, because we met a lot of beasts going to the Annual County Agricultural Show.'

As it happened, the critics of the motor car had a champion in the Chief Constable, for Colonel Daniell was a dedicated horseman. At one time, he even considered bicycles to be dangerous. When some of his constables were issued with the machines in 1896 to catch *scorchers* (speeding cyclists) on the Great North Road, he decided that the operation was sufficiently dangerous to justify awarding his men an extra 3d. an hour danger money! Little wonder, then, that the colonel, while a very fair-minded man, set out to offer the horse-owning majority as much protection from the motor car as the Law allowed.

Although in his first two years of motoring Sir Kenneth received his fair share of personal abuse from the public, it was an incident which occurred on a main street in Hertford which almost certainly drove home the need for a publicity campaign to help the public not only accept the motor car, but also to realise that it was here to stay. He was driving his de Dion at a sedate 8 miles an hour when an elderly woman started to cross the road about ten yards ahead of him. When she saw the car coming she let out a wail, clasped her hands together and fell face downwards to the ground. There she remained motionless, apparently resigned to the fate of being crushed to death by the monster that was bearing down upon her. In fact, Sir Kenneth stopped easily several feet short of the 'body', which remained motionless for several more moments before the old lady finally rose, dazed and quite unable to believe that she was still alive.

So, in conjunction with the Automobile Club, the Mayor of

'We were all outlaws...' Kenneth Murchison at the tiller of his De Bion-Bouton Voiturette.

Hertford set about arranging an Automobile Demonstration on the streets of the county town, which, he hoped would prove 'how slowly motors could go, and how quickly they could stop'. The week before the demonstration, the *Hertfordshire Mercury* carried a letter from the Mayor to warn the public of the event, 'in order that those whose horses are afraid of motor cars may know that there will be, if fine, a good many cars in and about the town that day. Also, that there may be a good many people who would like to avail themselves of this opportunity to accustom their horses to motors, standing still or in motion.'

Sir Kenneth also invited the Chief Constable to lunch with him and other members of the Automobile Club before the demonstration, and to propose the toast 'The Progress and Welfare of Automobilism'. Colonel Daniell accepted gracefully and, during his speech, put forward the interesting idea that cars of motorists convicted of reckless driving should be made to carry some special identification 'which would be an indication that the driver was a suspected character and would cause his driving to be more closely supervised by the police'.

The demonstration, which attracted some thirty cars from all over the country, was a great success, not least the event which involved a series of comparative braking contests between a car and a horse-drawn vehicle. There were gasps of surprise from the crowd when, on every occasion and despite their higher speeds, the cars proved to have the more efficient brakes. When the time came for Sir Kenneth to demonstrate his own vehicle, he chose a steep hill leading down into the town and invited the wary Chief Constable to join him as a passenger.

'Just as we started,' Sir Kenneth recalled 'he gripped the side of the car firmly and said "You be careful and remember I'm an old man". I remember going down the hill as quickly as I could – he looked as though we were going to shoot the rapids at Niagara. Having had my brakes smothered with French chalk I knew I could pull up in a very short distance: I must have been going between 25 and 28 miles an hour when the signal, a dropped handkerchief, was unexpectedly given half-way down the hill; a few yards sufficed in which to bring the de Dion to a standstill. The result was received with tumultuous applause by the watching crowd.'

In its journal the following month, the Automobile Club reported: 'That Hertfordshire will prove a paradise for motor cars is certain so long as drivers pay due consideration to other users of the road, and only drive at higher speeds on perfectly open and unoccupied roads. The police are very reasonable and favourably disposed towards motorists, two of them even going so far as to assist one of the visitors who had the misfortune to puncture, with a repair to his tyres.'

Of course, despite Sir Kenneth's thoughtful P.R. exercise, it was only a matter of time before the chief constable's worst fears were justified.

On 30th April, 1906, shortly before mid-day, a motor car crossed the border into Hertfordshire. It was a beautiful car, an 18 horse-power Peugeot, fashioned by French engineers and coach-builders with all the elegance of the Edwardian period. It had a mass of gleaming brass fittings and the coachwork of dark green and varnished wood was built in the Brougham style, making it reminiscent of the enclosed horse-drawn carriage which is was replacing. The upholstery was of buttoned leather, the windows of the enclosed rear compartment were fitted with dainty lace curtains and there was an electric light and a speaking tube, through which the occupants could issue instructions to their chauffeur. There was nobody in the rear compartment on this day; the sole passenger was sitting alongside the driver on the open front seat, protected only by a plate-glass windscreen.

Charles Preston, aged 52, 'a gentleman of Lancaster', was travelling south to London in a car owned by his cousin, and driven by her chauffeur, Albert Carter, aged 31, from Ashford. They had left Lancaster the day before, stopping overnight in Coventry before beginning the final stage of their journey down the old Watling Street to London. Carter, an experienced chauffeur, had driven some 75,000 miles during the three years in which he had held his licence. That day, he had been at the wheel for about two and a half hours as they passed through the village of Markyate and on towards St Albans.

At about the same time, a mile or so further south, two other men were beginning a more routine journey. Horace Pedder and his brother Alfred of Flamstead village, were making their way down Pepperstock Lane towards the London road, each in charge of a horse and cart. They were on their way to load up with animal fodder which they were due to cart to London later that day. At the junction of the lane with the main road, Horace was in front leading his horse on foot. He was half-way across the main road when he heard his brother shout, but it was too late.

The Peugeot hit them broadside on, pushing the heavy cart and stricken animal twenty yards up the road and throwing Horace Pedder onto the grass verge. The sight which confronted the rescuers was not pleasant. Horace Pedder was screaming with the pain from two broken legs. The horse, lying in a tangle of broken shafts and harness, was so badly injured it had to be destroyed. Albert Carter, the chauffeur, apparently protected to a degree by his leather-covered steering wheel, had only superficial

The scene near Markyate after the collision. The horse lies dying and, behind the overturned wagon, a group stands watching a doctor tend the victim, Charles Preston.

injuries and was kneeling beside his passenger, who had been less fortunate. Charles Preston had been thrown forward violently by the impact of the collision; his face had been torn dreadfully by the glass of the windscreen and his jaw, nose and skull shattered on impact with the heavy wooden cart.

Within a short time a policeman, a doctor and a clergyman were on the scene. They put splints on the injured wagon man and carefully carried Charles Preston across to a nearby public house which, ironically, bore the name *The Waggon and Horses*. Preston, despite his terrible injuries, was conscious for some time and repeatedly asked the same question, 'Were we to blame?' It was a question which he never heard answered, for he died that night at the West Hertfordshire Infirmary. Meanwhile, for his distressed chauffeur there began an ordeal which lasted for three months, as the machinery of the law was set into motion to try to find the answer to the question asked by his dying passenger.

There was no worse place in England for Albert Carter to have been involved in such an accident at such a time. For Markyate were still recovering from the death, a year earlier, of little Willie Clifton, aged 4, after he had been struck down in the High Street by a car which had failed to stop. It was the first hit-and-run fatality ever known in England and it had caused a national furore. So much so that Sir Alfred Harmsworth, proprietor of the *Daily Mail*, offered a reward of £100 for information leading to the discovery of the vehicle.

The money was never paid because of what the *Daily Mail* later referred to as 'one of the most amazing coincidences on record'; the owner of the elusive car turned out to be none other than Sir Alfred's brother, Mr Hildebrand Harmsworth! No member of the Harmsworth family was in the car at the time and it was only after Mr Harmsworth himself had read the story and initiated enquiries with Scotland Yard and the Hertfordshire police that the full story emerged. Harmsworth's chauffeur, a Spaniard named Rocco Cornalbas, had been driving two of his employer's friends to London when the accident happened. Thinking he had caught the little boy 'only a light, glancing blow', Cornalbas decided he had probably not been hurt and had driven on. At least, that was his story when he stood trial for manslaughter at Hertfordshire Assizes in July 1905. He was found guilty and sentenced to six months' hard labour.

Now, less than a year later, a second chauffeur faced a similar charge. Albert Carter was accused of the manslaughter of his passenger. At his trial, as at the inquest on Charles Preston, the outcome hinged almost entirely upon estimates of the speed at which the Peugeot had been travelling immediately before the collision with the horse and cart. On this, there was considerable disagreement. Some claimed the Peugeot went through Markyate's High Street at between 20 and 30 miles an hour. The landlord of the *Green Man* said it went past his pub 'like a flash of lightning'. Others said the speed was much lower than that, and blamed the wagoner, Horace Pedder, for completely misjudging the speed of the car before leading his horse and cart out into the road.

Carter himself said he was travelling at between 15 and 18 miles an hour just prior to the crash and claimed he had been sounding his horn all the way along the road. However, under

A crossroads encounter at St Albans in 1912 which resulted in each driver being fined £5 for careless driving.

cross-examination, he agreed that – having travelled the 62 miles from Coventry to Markyate in just under two and a half hours – his average speed for the journey must have been at least 23 miles an hour. It was probably that admission which led the jury to reach a verdict of Guilty, with a strong recommendation for leniency in view of Carter's good record. That recommendation was reflected in the sentence of two months' imprisonment imposed on the chauffeur at Hertfordshire Assizes on 6th July, 1906.

The conclusion of that trial enabled Hertfordshire Police to close their file on what became known as The Markyate Motor Tragedies. Yet, while closing a file, they were in fact opening a whole new book. For this had been their first taste of a new and hideous event which was to be repeated as many as a hundred times a year upon the roads of Hertfordshire: Death by Motor Vehicle.

Twenty Thousand Shillings

★

Even parsons have nightmares. A common one is experienced during difficult fund-raising campaigns when the good men, trying to find sufficient cash for urgent church repairs become susceptible to nocturnal visions of God's House falling down about them. The Reverend Ralph Lindsay Loughborough suffered such a vision in 1875. His church fell down and, unfortunately, it was not in a dream.

In 1851, when the population was flocking to London to see the marvels of Victorian achievement on display at the Prince Consort's great Crystal Palace Exhibition in Hyde Park, Mr Loughborough left the capital and brought his wife to a new and humble living in Hertfordshire – where many of the less wonderful aspects of Victorian life were still on display. He brought her to the village of Pirton, a far cry from their cosy living in South London, which demanded of them qualities approaching those of a missionary building a church in a foreign land. Loughborough's problem was that he was the first resident vicar to be appointed to Pirton for more than two hundred years and during the whole of that time the village, with its large and impressive Norman church, had been incorporated with the neighbouring parish of Ickleford, three miles away. There, successive rectors, pre-occupied with their own affairs, had allowed Pirton and the church to become a neglected satellite where parishioners had to organise their own service as best they could and where Holy Communion was celebrated only three times a year by a curate who had to trudge across the fields from Ickleford. curate who had to trudge across the fields from Ickleford.

The parson, who had even to build his own vicarage before he could move to Pirton, soon discovered that the church of St

The Rev Ralph Loughborough towards the end of his forty-year ministry as first Vicar of Pirton.

41

Mary had crumbled away to a condition that invited disaster. The south transept, which formed the right arm of the cruciform plan, had already collapsed, and the vestry was a damp little wooden hut leaning against the wall of the tall tower which itself was showing some alarming cracks. The only repairs carried out had been of a make-shift character, the more ominous holes having been hastily filled with mortar and hidden with plaster and brickwork.

Ralph Loughborough tried to launch a fund-raising scheme among his parishioners but his efforts were futile. The plain fact was that they had no money. Of a population of 1,100, all but a handful were families with an average income of £1 a week, the men working as farm labourers, the women and children supplementing the family income by straw-plaiting. Neither was there a wealthy squire nor any other landowner living in the parish who might be persuaded to make a large contribution towards the restoration of St Mary's Church. Nevertheless, early in 1871, the vicar decided to call in an eminent London church architect, J.L. Pearson, to survey St Mary's and put forward estimates for the restoration. Pearson reported that the collapse of the south transept earlier had weakened the tower, which would need to be strengthened before the transept could be rebuilt. He also discovered that the roof above the nave was in a dangerous state and would have to be completely replaced; a project which would cost the then enormous sum of £2,000. In fact, the situation was to prove even worse than the experienced architect had predicted.

Since their own parishioners had no money, Ralph and Marianna Loughborough decided to direct their money-raising campaign towards the neighbouring towns and parishes in the diocese. Night after night they spent hours at their desks, writing personal letters and composing appeal leaflets and advertisements. At the end of a few weeks, there was hardly a bishop, a priest or businessman who was not aware of the appalling state of St Mary's Church. Loughborough didn't mince his words in these letters: 'There is no vestry, nor other convenience for the officiating minister,' he wrote. 'The font, prayer desk, pulpit and doors are of the commonest description and utterly unworthy of the

House of God.' This spirited campaign inevitably attracted the attention of the Press; a correspondent of the *Hertfordshire Express* went to see things for himself and returned to pen indignantly: 'Time and the ignorance and barbarism of past generations have well-nigh done their worst to efface the comeliness of God's House. There are doors, windows, fittings and appliances that no man of ordinary respectability would think good enough to call his own.'

By this time the 'gentleman parson' had become more than a spiritual leader to the people of Pirton. The tall man, with his fierce beard and forceful personality, epitomised the sort of man who dominated life in most other villages at that time. So the village boys bowed and the little girls curtsied when Mr Loughborough and his lady went past and the elder ones christened him 'The Squire'. The local Baptists, on the other hand, treated him with rather less respect, having become firmly established during the years in which St Mary's had no resident parson. They took great exception to his bombastic pulpit-thumping and their lay-preachers frequently waylaid him and attempted to 'expose his wrong teaching'. The bigotry and religious intolerance displayed by both sides resulted in many fierce arguments, Loughborough throwing eloquent bible quotations in support of his beliefs, only to find himself ducking a return volley of fresh ones that put the Baptist case equally effectively. According to the Baptists the Vicar, at this point, was obliged to cover his retreat by resorting to quotations from the 'unknown languages' of Greek and Latin of which, conveniently, he was the village's only exponent.

Nevertheless, he commanded tremendous respect from his own flock and when the time came in 1875 to begin the repair work on the church, there was no shortage of volunteers; the poor came forward and offered their time and energy in lieu of money. The team that began the repair work had been warned that the sixty foot tower of St Mary's was unsafe, so it was with some caution that they began to peck at the area around the base, intending to replace the crumbling stone with fresh blocks of clunchstone quarried from the local pit. Hardly had the first pick-axe been driven in when the workmen became aware of

The service to launch the re-building of St Mary's Church, Pirton, following the collapse of its tower in 1875.

movement. Then, in the words of a witness, 'the whole lower portion of the tower came away, rushing down like a stream of water'. By the grace of God, presumably, the top section of the tower was made of stronger material, having apparently been re-built two or three hundred years after the original base and so, incredibly, it did not fall but remained there suspended precariously between the upper walls and roof of the nave and chancel.

The disaster meant, of course, a complete revision of plans. Far from damaging morale, the incident served to strengthen the determination of those involved. The top of the tower was quickly demolished and plans for the construction of the south transept were abandoned so that all effort could be concentrated on re-building the huge tower. Tons more fresh clunch-stone had to

44

be quarried while the masons salvaged as much as they could from the ruins of the old tower.

In July 1876, a dozen clergymen and other guests from the neighbouring parishes which had supported the appeal gathered with the villagers and workmen for a service to commemorate the laying of the corner-stone to the new tower. It seems difficult to believe that just six months later, on a frosty January Sunday, the tower was restored and re-opened to a joyous peal of bells, a sound which had not been heard in Pirton for very many years.

Meanwhile the campaign for money – which had already been running for six years – was resumed with renewed vigour. Loughborough's wife, Marianna, achieved a most remarkable coup with an imaginative advertisement placed in the columns of *The Times* newspaper.

TWENTY THOUSAND SHILLINGS – Who will help? a clergyman's wife WANTS to raise the SUM to assist in the reparation of a large church in the midst of a poor rural community. Tower so unsafe had to be taken down; rest of building much decayed. Please send one shilling to Mrs Loughborough, Pirton Vicarage, near Hitchin.

The response was remarkable. From the length and breadth of England, and from Scotland, too, the shillings cascaded in. Hundreds of them, each to be recorded meticulously by the vicar in his Restoration Fund accounts book. In the end, the couple raised more than £3,000, which was sufficient to repair the church and re-furnish the interior. Ralph Loughborough died in 1895 at the age of 76, and Marianna twelve years later. After her funeral, the new vicar and the wardens of this now thriving parish church had little difficulty in deciding upon a memorial. They would build the south transept which Ralph Loughborough had planned but had been forced to abandon because of the collapse of the tower.

Once again the volunteers came forward – seventy men and boys from the village – who, over a period of six years, quarried sufficient clunch-stone to build the transept. The walls, three feet thick, required one hundred and fifty cart-loads of

45

St Mary's, Pirton, after its restoration.

material. Much of the work, the masonry, the carpentry, the plumbing and the carting, was done free of charge. The wives raised money for a tracery window, the children collected for a new oak door. The transept was completed and opened as a vestry in 1913:

'A memorial to Ralph Lindsay Loughborough, first sole Vicar of Pirton, and his wife Marianna. Two servants of God who laboured in Pirton for nearly half a century and who were lovingly enshrined in the hearts of those they left behind.'

46

The Scandal of the Poor

★

At the turn of the century the North Hertfordshire market town of Hitchin was a town of contrasts. As one the country's main centres of lavender cultivation it was frequently featured in the fashion columns and journals of the day as 'the town of sweet smells' to which ladies came from far and wide to purchase the latest exotic examples of Mr Sam Perks' Lavender Water, soaps, and oils. The many acres of lavender fields were themselves a major attraction which brought hundreds of tourists to the town each summer. 'I will never erase from my mind,' enthused one such visitor, 'the impression made by coming suddenly upon a great expanse clothed with lavender in full blossom, cultivated to the extreme height of floral productiveness, and with no other tint to break the broad, level rich blue-grey blaze.'

However, less than two hundred yards from Messrs Perks and Llewellyn's fragrant High Street emporium through the church-yard, past St Mary's Church and on the other side of the River Hiz, stood the town's least-prestigious contribution to the Victorian and Edwardian social scene. For most other residents of Hitchin the Queen Street slums were, to use the modern idiom, a no-go area; two or three acres of land on which huddled hundreds of crumbling cottages. Into these were crammed the poor, the inadequate, the criminal, and all others to whom that notable Victorian euphemism 'the rougher element' was normally applied. It was a district where policemen always patrolled in pairs and into which nobody who was not a resident liked to venture after dark. A small sore, admittedly, compared with the vast slum malignancies of the industrial cities, but one which was evident in every small town and which contributed to the Victorian housing scandal.

It is true that politicians had begun to tackle the problem of poor housing as early as the 1850s, with the passing of the first Public Health Acts, but it was not until 1875 that housing legis-

47

A corner of the Queen Street slum area, Hitchin, in 1900.

lation was put onto a really sound foundation with the first laws which obliged slum landlords to either repair their properties or to demolish them, or face compulsory purchase orders from the local authorities. Even so, improvements were far from immediate and it was to be another fifty years before slum neighbourhoods such as the one in Hitchin began to disappear for good.

The Queen Street slums were made up of dozens of little cobbled courtyards leading off the main street every few yards: Chapman's Yard, Gascoigne's Yard, Webb's Yard, Thorpe's Yard, Peahen Yard, Barnard's Yard. Each had a couple of dozen tiny cottages, the same one-up-one-down hovels as those inhabited by the farm workers but packed far more tightly together and with no gardens. Some had earth floors and each group of twenty-four families had to share a single cold water tap which stood in the centre of the yard. Also shared were the one or two earth closets tucked away in a corner. These were the people for whom Victorian social reformers were fighting in what was known as

48

the battle of the pig and sty, acknowledging, in other words, that if Society insisted that some of its people should live in homes little better than pig-sties, then Society should not be surprised if they started behaving like swine.

In fact, many good families lived there, who though poor, were hard-working. The men laboured on the railway or at the local tannery, the women did seasonal work such as straw-plaiting helping with the lavender cultivation or picking dandelions and other suitable wild plants which could be sold to William Ransome's distillery. Inevitably it was a very tough area; there were thirteen public houses, which along with the inhuman and over-crowded living conditions did much to provoke drunkenness, fighting and domestic disputes.

In the autumn of 1904, the owner of a block of these cottages in Barnard's Yard applied to the Hitchin Justices for eviction orders against a number of families upon whom he had served notices to quit, but who had refused to go. The case attracted little interest, the local newspaper reporting only briefly that the landlord wished to renovate the property and that the tenants (whom they did not bother to name) had been unable to find alternative accommodation. Their plea was borne out by Police Superintendent John Reynolds, who told the Court that, as far as he knew, there were no other cottages to let in the town. The justices granted the eviction orders, suspending them for a further four weeks so that the families might have more time to find other homes, but on the day the orders were served, 5th October, 1904, they were still there, and the police and bailiffs had to evict them forcibly. A brief but revealing account of the event appeared in the *Hertfordshire Express* the following Saturday:

'Some unusual scenes were witnessed in Queen Street on Wednesday when, under ejectment orders issued a month ago, Superintendent Reynolds and a number of constables removed the goods and chattels of a number of cottagers living in Barnard's Yard. For years the yard has been a cause of much difficulty owing to its insanitary state and the conditions under which the occupants have to live. Soon after ten o'clock the work began to the accompaniment of profuse anathemas hurled at the police, who had a very disagreeable task. Other things than furniture

49

were found in the houses and as, in addition, some of the occupiers had been keeping poultry, pigeons and even a horse indoors, conditions were not of the most salubrious. The property was speedily removed and the erstwhile tenants had to survey their household goods in the open air. But neighbouring barns were quickly at their disposal and cover was found. A photographer (Mr H. G. Moulden) wishing to depict the scene had a rough time and had to be protected by the police as he went about his work. The important question left was how to deal with the eight people thus left homeless, and with the usual generosity of their class the neighbours solved it by taking in the outcasts.'

The last point illustrates one of the main reasons why, despite earlier legislation, the slum situation got worse in some places before it got better. It was all very well to demolish or restore decaying property, but those who lost their homes because of it were too poor to afford anything better, so the only course open to them was to seek refuge in other slums, which simply increased overcrowding and worsened living conditions elsewhere. The First World War made the situation worse by putting a virtual stop to all public and private building and in 1917, when the problem had reached crisis point, a Royal Commission blamed the appalling conditions of working class homes not only for the industrial unrest but also for the alarming state of health of the poorer children. Of nearly two and a half million school children medically examined, nearly half were physically defective. Only after the signing of the Armistice did Parliament and people unite in a common pledge to build homes 'fit for heroes to live in'. Important reforms followed quickly which, while not without their imperfections, enabled local authorities to go ahead with schemes for estates of council houses, the government covering the additional costs caused by higher wages and prices.

The Queen Street slums disappeared for good in the 1920s, their remains buried beneath the new town square which was named St Mary's Square after the church which it overlooks. The town council left an inscription on the steps which lead up to it from the River Hiz:

'On the adjacent area formerly stood 174 cottages, which were

50

demolished under slum clearance schemes and the occupants, 637 in number, housed elsewhere.
A.D. 1925-29.'

This was a considerable social achievement for a town the size of Hitchin. For the majority of the poor, life was a long tragedy, and as the following history indicates, for many domestic service was the only future.

Alice was only 5 years old when they came to take her away from her family. It was a painful moment and she cried a lot, but the report of the inspector emphasised the urgency of the situation. 'The family lives in the very worst conditions in a slum cottage in Clerkenwell and the widowed mother contacted our representative in a state of great distress. She works as a cook and her wages are such that she is quite unable to support her five children. Consumption is a bad heritage. The father died from it, the oldest son and a daughter are smitten with it. The little girl, however, may be saved and probably will with six or seven years of country life and air'.

So, on a summer afternoon in 1908, a kindly lady from the society calling itself The National Refuges for Homeless and Destitute Children, took Alice away from London and her sick family and brought her to Hertfordshire. The little girl was one of a number whose destinies were changed that summer, for Alice had become one of the first children to go to a new home which the Society had opened at Royston, as the first of its kind to cater specifically for little girls between the ages of 5 and 10. It was another step forward by the organisation founded originally in 1843 to open *ragged schools* for destitute children in the City of London, which was later amalgamated with the Earl of Shaftesbury's Arethusa Training Ship Scheme for homeless boys to become the *Shaftesbury Homes and Arethusa*.

At the turn of the century, the National Refuges for Homeless and Destitute Children had more than a thousand boys and girls in its care and yet was worried by the fact that it consistently had to refuse small girls like Alice because there was nowhere suitable for them to live. For this reason the society bought a five-acre site on a chalk ridge overlooking Royston and built *The Home*

51

for Little Girls. It was a combined home and school for eighty youngsters and run by a staff of three, a matron and two teachers, who between them commanded salaries which totalled just under £350 a year. The youngsters taken to the home that summer were victims, not simply of poverty, but of disease, malnutrition and ill-treatment. The health risks involved in bringing so many of them together under one roof so suddenly were considerable and, consequently, initial medical precautions taken by the matron were drastic. The head of each little girl was shaved and the hair burnt, and those found to be infected with lice were treated daily in baths of disinfectant, and for a short period of time each child had a weekly medical examination by a local doctor.

It was all to good effect, since a few weeks later in his first report on the school, the local inspector, Mr Wix, found: 'The children are very orderly and delightfully happy and natural. Both divisions are taught with much thought and care and the school has made a promising start in excellent and well-equipped premises, where the children are under the influence of a good school and a happy well-ordered home.' Alice remained at Royston for five years until she was old enough to be transferred to the society's home at Ealing where, from the age of 10, she began to receive the training and discipline considered necessary to prepare for the only respectable and secure station in life then available for a girl in her position – domestic service. The training was described by the matron of the Ealing home in her report to the governors in the year that Alice reached her fifteenth birthday.

'So much has to be done in the way of mental health and moral instruction that it is manifest that a complete training in household work is impossible; but, as far as our means allow, the committee do the best that is possible. All the work at the home is done by the girls – sweeping, scrubbing, washing, dormitory work, cooking and sewing, and as each girl's period of residence is drawing to a close at the age of 15 they are subjected to special training fitting them for housemaid's work, some for the kitchen or the scullery according to their capabilities and leanings. Out of 40 girls discharged during the year 33 went into service, so that subscribers may feel assured that the training which has been given is really of value to the girls.'

52

First occupants of The Home for Little Girls, at Royston, in 1908, some still showing evidence of the mandatory head-shaving as a precaution against lice.

The following year, when she was approaching her seventeenth birthday, Alice wrote a letter to her old matron on notepaper bearing a fashionable address in Hampstead, London.

'Dear Matron,
    I hope you are quite well and all the teachers. I know you will be pleased to hear that I am still getting on. I had my second rise, making me £14 a year. I hope the measles at the school has quite gone by now, they always were such a worry to you. All being well I shall come to Old Girls' Reunion next Thursday week. It seems such a long time since I was at the dear old place. I sometimes wish I could come back again.
    I remain, dearest matron, one of your Old Girls,
                                                        Alice.'

The Poachers

★

Only Charles Dickens would have dared to invent such a pair –
a brace of poachers, twin brothers, who shared the name of Fox!
Yet, as gamekeepers, policemen and magistrates in North
Hertfordshire came to learn, these characters were very much
alive; a couple of likeable villains who between them managed
to notch up two hundred convictions and whose nocturnal activities made them a legend in their own lifetime. They even
earned themselves a modest space on the wall of Scotland Yard's
Black Museum where, billed as *The Most Infamous Poachers of All
Time,* they offer a modicum of light relief to an otherwise grisly
show.

The Fox twins were born in the autumn of 1857 to Henry
and Charlotte Fox, of Ten Acre Farm, Symond's Green, near
Stevenage. Henry was reputedly descended from George Fox,
the founder of the Quaker Society of Friends, and was a deeply
religious man who had earned a good reputation as a preacher.
He was also a regular worshipper at the Ebenezer Strict Baptist
Chapel in Albert Street, Stevenage, which presumably prompted
him in a moment of devout loyalty to christen his boys Ebenezer
Albert and Albert Ebenezer. As it was, by giving his identical
sons almost identical names, their father innocently helped them
to escape almost as many charges as they were convicted on.

Albert and Ebenezer began to learn about and love the country
almost as soon as they could walk; their lusting after its forbidden
fruits emerged not long afterwards. By the time they were 10
they knew every copse and meadow for miles around their little
farmstead. At the age of 11, they left school and were found jobs
on neighbouring farms but they didn't like them. The same year,
they set a gin-trap and caught their first rabbit. In 1871, at the
age of 14, they were caught by a gamekeeper, poaching on his
estate with a stolen gun. Henry Fox did the best he could for

54

A shooting party of Hertfordshire sportsmen at Whomerly Wood, Stevenage, in 1894. The wood was a favourite poaching haunt of the Fox twins and Gamekeeper Keene (standing, extreme left) one of their deadliest foes.

his sons; he engaged a solicitor who pleaded that the two innocent lads were only indulging in an isolated, if misguided, prank and should never have been prosecuted. The magistrate on the Hitchin bench agreed and the boys were let off. A month later, the same gamekeeper caught them again and they appeared before the same magistrate on the same charge – this time without a solicitor. A 10s. 0d. fine was recorded, the first of a list of poaching convictions that ended nearly seventy years later when the last of the twin Foxes was called to earth.

During that period Ebenezer collected eighty-two convictions and Albert one hundred and eighteen; the difference accounted for by the fact that Albert survived his brother by nearly twelve years. The twins also lost vast amounts of equipment, confiscated by the courts; more than fifty guns, ranging from flint-locks to

55

Before the trouble started. Henry Fox, respected farmer and Baptist preacher, photographed with his twin sons in the 1860s when Albert and Ebenezer were about ten years old.

56

muzzle and breech-loaders, hundreds of snares and traps, scores of yards of silk netting (to trap pheasant and partridge) and around five hundred yards of string netting (for rabbits). They always worked with a lurcher, a cross between a greyhound and a sheepdog, the combined characteristics of which made it ideal for poaching. Working with a lurcher, they once netted a thousands rabbits in one month. At night, they worked with the foresights of their guns either covered with white chalk or tipped with the head of a lucifer match which gave a small luminous glow when dampened. Albert, who emerged the stronger and better-natured of the twins, was also the better shot. He once bagged eight pheasants with one barrel but, at the same time, could kill cleanly when he wanted, bringing down a bird with just one or two pellets from the extreme edge of his spread of grapeshot.

Inevitably, with each succeeding court case, the twins' poaching reputation was further enhanced. Magistrates were often held spellbound, not only by the evidence of the police and gamekeepers but also by the highly imaginative defence pleas submitted by the defendants. Each time they appeared before the bench they maintained a well-practised attitude of hurt innocence. They were short stout men, just five feet two inches high with gnome-like figures and puckish faces of weather-beaten mahogany brown to match. Ebenezer, caught once in Hitch Wood, Preston, at dead of night, after first managing successfully to hide his gun and his bag, was nevertheless brought before the Hitchin bench the following Tuesday. 'All right Fox,' said the Chairman. 'I acknowledge you were without game or gun when arrested. But can you tell me why you were there, in a wood at dead of night, if not for an illegal purpose?'

'The truth was sir', replied Ebenezer, 'I was there to meditate upon the Baptist hymn book'. While the court clutched its sides for several minutes, Ebenezer, displaying some annoyance at the hilarity, delved angrily into the deep pocket of his black poaching coat. After rummaging around for several minutes he finally held aloft in triumph and amid a small cloud of feathers! the Baptist hymn book which his father had given him as a boy.

The twins' only really successful defence was that of mistaken

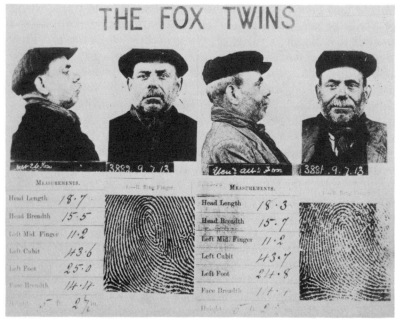

1913 'mug-shots' from police records show how the Law was eventually able to distinguish one Fox twin from the othr without going through the laborious Bertillon system of measuring height, hands and feet. Prints taken of the right ring finger of the twins are completely different.

identity. After a while, they took to poaching singly and, when caught, each gave the other's name instead of his own. The keepers, unable to tell one from the other, had to accept what they were given. Thus, when Albert appeared in court charged under his brother's name, he could ask for, and frequently got, a dismissal on the grounds of a technicality. Many times a policeman or a keeper hesitated in the box under cross-examination when asked by one of the twins whether he was absolutely sure it was the defendant and not his brother whom he had seen that night.

Sometimes it worked, sometimes it didn't. When it didn't there was usually a fine of a guinea or two or, if the twins weren't very flush at the time, a fortnight in gaol at Bedford, Hertford or St Albans. Their 'mistaken identity' plea was scuttled for good in 1901 when the Metropolitan Police Commissioner, Sir Edward

Henry, introduced finger-printing as a standard part of all criminal records. Within a year or two of the opening of Scotland Yard's finger-print department, the Home Counties followed suit and in 1904 the twins were among the first group of criminals in Britain to be convicted on corroborative evidence based on their finger-prints. Albert and Ebenezer accepted all this with good heart, as they did their fines and imprisonment. It was one reason why they became so popular; gamekeepers, policemen and magistrates all agreed, they were always courteous – two of the most courteous liars they had ever come across.

Their charm, no doubt, was the main reason why they developed a considerable rapport with the local landed gentry whose preserves in North and Mid-Hertfordshire they regularly poached. One lady of the manor, well aware of Alberts devastating nightly exploits into her game preserves, even resorted to offering him protection money, approaching him personally at the opening of the pheasant season with the promise of a sovereign a week and a brace of pheasant, provided he agreed to keep off her land. The proposition was too good to turn down; Albert accepted gracefully and kept his word – leaving brother Ebenezer to poach the good lady's land on his own that winter! It was the ever-resourceful Albert who, when fined £1 by the St Albans bench for poaching, respectfully asked for twenty-four hours in which to find the money. The request granted, he spent that night on the estate owned by the magistrate who had imposed the fine. Next morning he turned up at St Albans Market with several brace of pheasant which he disposed of in no time. He then marched round to the offices of the Justices's Clerk, paid his fine and set off back to Stevenage and home. Home for the twins, after their parents' farmhouse fell into decay through neglect, was a primitive gipsy-type hut which they built for themselves entirely from twigs, branches and turf. They called it *Woodbine Cottage*.

By the year 1915, when Albert chalked up his hundredth poaching conviction, the twins' career had reached a peak. They chose to celebrate it with a rare period of honest wage earning, working for several weeks as hod-and-mortar carriers for the men building a new and impressive edifice in the centre of Stevenage. It was

The poachers enjoying a brief spell of honest work – helping to build Stevenage Police Station.

an irony which the locals could scarcely ignore, for Albert and Ebenezer were helping to build the new police station and magistrates' court. So the *North Herts Mail,* only weeks after recording Albert's 'century', was moved to feature the twins again, picturing them this time at work on the cells which, in fact, they later became the first to occupy! It is perhaps an indication of the affection which these old rascals enjoyed that the newspapers did not stoop so low as to refer to them as poachers, but as 'those genial sporting gentlemen who are familiar figures in the local courts on Game Law summonses'.

The twins could also claim to have a Royal Seal of Approval, if not on their poaching activities, then certainly on their skill as shots. It was placed upon Albert by that other genial sporting gentlemen, Edward, Prince of Wales (later King Edward VII), in the public bar of the *Marquis of Lorne* one summer lunchtime in 1900. The Prince was motoring to Newmarket races when his car broke down in Stevenage High Street and while the repairs were carried out, he spent half an hour in the pub, during which time Albert was introduced to him. Far from being overwhelmed by the occasion, Albert recognised a fellow sportsman and was soon swapping yarns with him. It is said that when the Prince's equerry returned to the pub to tell Edward that the repairs to his car were completed, the Prince introduced Albert to him as 'a man who can shoot more birds by moonlight than you have shot by day'.

It is not difficult to understand why they were so popular; the crime they chose to live by may once have been punishable by hanging, but it is also the crime which appeals most to the man frustrated by the trappings of civilisation. A comparatively harmless crime which demands of the perpetrator all the basic instincts and qualities of Man the Hunter; an absolute knowledge of the wild animal and its territory, stealth, cunning, courage, a sharp eye and a cool nerve. The Fox twins had all these qualities and so were quietly envied and admired.

It was a pity, then, that Ebenezer should have tarnished their sporting reputation by committing a vicious and uncharacteristic crime, by inflicting grievous bodily harm upon a gamekeeper who caught him at work during a night poaching exercise. It was always reckoned that Ebenezer was the weaker of the two, the one who panicked when they were on the run, and it was this panic that caused him to lash out when he found himself trapped. He paid dearly for the mistake, receiving a sentence of ten years' penal servitude from the judge at Hertfordshire Assizes.

When they finally let him out he was an old man. He tried a job or two and started going regularly to the Baptist Chapel from which he had received his name. He even tried poaching again but found he was too deaf to work efficiently any more. Eventually, in his late sixties, he could look after himself no more and was taken to the Hitchin Infirmary at the old Chalkdell Workhouse. In September 1926, he became aware that he was dying, and clearly made up his mind that he wasn't going to do that in the unaccustomed comfort of a hospital ward under the public gaze of attendant doctors and nurses. So, dressed in pyjamas of hospital blue, he stole out one night and made off towards his old hunting territory. He got through Hitchin and half-way towards his birthplace at Symond's Green before his tired legs gave out. He managed to crawl into a woodland thicket and was found there three days later. At Ebenezer's inquest, the coroner recorded a verdict of death from exposure and exhaustion.

Albert went on poaching and lived to enjoy his 80th year before he, too was taken to the infirmary to die. Many old friends and enemies turned up to see him buried near his brother in St Nicholas churchyard, Stevenage. Those who couldn't come sent wreaths – landowners he had robbed, a magistrate who had sent him down, Baptists who had prayed for him and poulterers who had been his receivers. All had their feelings adequately summed up by the verse that accompanied a wreath from the Hitchin lawyer and historian, Reginald Hine:

'Gone to earth old friend
And lost to mortal view.
Good luck to you where'er you wend
Fresh woods and pastures new.'

Shall Mary Ansell Die?

★

The young servant girl gazed impassively at the judge as the black cap was placed upon his head. Mary Ansell, aged 22, was small, stocky and very plain. Only her head could be seen above the spiked rim of the dock at Hertfordshire Assize Court as Mr Justice Mathew intoned upon the enormity of her crime. 'Never in my experience has so terrible a crime been committed for a motive so utterly inadequate,' he said. 'Do not hope for any mercy in this world.' Mary did not ask for any mercy and as sentence of death was passed upon her she remained as she had been throughout her trial – almost indifferent to the proceedings, calmly but firmly denying that it was she who had posted the poisoned cake to her sister.

The parcel containing the deadly present had arrived at Leavesden Lunatic Asylum, near Watford, on March 9th 1899, addressed to Mary's sister Caroline, who was a patient in Ward 7. Caroline was 26 and had been at Leavesden for four years. As was the custom the parcel had been opened by one of the staff and its contents examined before being passed to the patient. Charge nurse Alice Felmingham said the cake – a small flat sandwich – had seemed perfectly normal, although the filling which formed the centre layer was 'very yellow'. The next day Caroline ate half the cake herself and shared the remainder with four fellow inmates. One immediately spat out her portion, complaining that it tasted bitter, and was sick shortly afterwards. The others ate theirs and later, after experiencing violent stomach pains, also vomited several times. The following day all, including Caroline, appeared to have recovered sufficiently to enjoy a Sunday lunch of roast beef. However, two days later, Caroline fell seriously ill and was transferred to the asylum's infirmary suffering from even more excruciating abdominal pains. After several hours of agony, she fell into a coma and died the same evening.

63

For a time there was no suspicion that this was a case of murder. The asylum's Medical Superintendent Henry Elkins and his deputy Dr Cameron Blair were both convinced that Caroline had died from peritonitis. It was only when the nurses recalled how ill some of the other patients had been after sharing Caroline's cake that the doctors decided to approach the dead girl's family to seek permission to perform a post mortem examination.

Although permission was refused, Dr Elkins and Dr Blair had also reported their suspicions to the Watford coroner and on his instructions a post mortem examination was carried out by an independent doctor. His findings, later confirmed by a leading Home Office pathologist, were that Caroline had died from phosphorous poisoning – a fact borne out by the state of some of the victim's organs and by the manner in which she had died. The pathologist Dr Thomas Stevenson explained that phosphorous acted somewhat differently to other poisons. It was a strong irritant poison and, when first taken, would produce sickness, nausea and internal irritation. The patient would seem to recover from this after about 24 hours and would feel quite well for two or three days but throughout this period the poison was attacking the kidneys and liver which would eventually collapse causing acute pain and jaundice from which the patient was unlikely to recover. It was a pattern of illness identical to that experienced by Caroline Ansell.

As the investigation proceeded under the direction of Police Superintendent William Wood, members of the asylum staff began to recall other incidents which had occurred during the weeks leading up to the poisoning. They remembered how, a month earlier, another parcel had arrived for Caroline, containing tea and sugar. They had used it the next day but had to throw the brew away the taste was so bitter. There had also been another strange episode at about the same time when charge nurse Felmingham had found Caroline crying over a letter she had received, supposedly from a cousin, informing her that her mother and father were dead, when they were both actually alive and well.

As the search went on for further clues P.C. Tom Piggott discovered on the asylum rubbish tip the brown paper wrapper in which the deadly cake had arrived. The wrapper bore a W.C.1.

postmark – the same postal area as the Ansell's house in Tankerton Street just off London's Gray's Inn Road.

Police enquiries elsewhere in London W.C.1. were beginning to uncover other interesting facts. For three years, Mary had been employed as a servant to a Mr and Mrs Patrick Maloney, who lived about half-a-mile away on the wealthier side of the same district, in Coram Street. Mr Maloney had an insurance policy with The Royal London Friendly Society and an agent of that society, John Cooper, had been in the habit of calling at the house once a month to collect the premium. In September 1898, about six months before the murder, Mary had suggested she might take out a policy on Caroline's life. She said her sister was 'a general servant' at Leavesden Asylum and was in good health. Rightly or wrongly the agent allowed Mary to sign the proposal form and put the wheels into motion without asking for any further evidence about the general welfare of her sister. A policy was eventually drawn up insuring Caroline's life for £22 10s 0d.

Since the policy had been in force only six months, the amount payable on Caroline's death was only half the sum insured – namely £11 5s 0d. It would seem pointless for Mary to insure her sister's life and then kill for her for such a small sum of money but this motive began to gather credibility when her employer, Mrs Margaret Maloney, disclosed that the servant-girl and her boyfriend had been planning to marry the following Easter but that the boyfriend had unexpectedly postponed 'the affair' saying he didn't want to get married until he was earning sufficient money to keep them both.

While working for the Maloneys, Mary had lived and slept in the kitchen area and it was when they were searching this part of the house that the police found their most important clue. On a shelf in the pantry they discovered a small jar of phosphorous paste – a rat poison – of a brand which could be purchased at most hardware shops. Mrs Maloney was sure she had never instructed Mary to buy any. Enquiries at a hardware shop in adjoining Marchmont Street gave Superintendent Wood the evidence he had been seeking for nearly a fortnight. The owner recalled that, during a period of three weeks in February and March, Mary Ansell had bought either three of four jars of the poison,

65

saying she needed it to get rid of rats in the cellar and kitchen of the Maloney's house. The Superintendent purchased a couple of jars himself and sent them to Dr Stevenson at Guys Hospital for official analysis. Each contained sufficient poison to kill at least three human beings.

On April 6th 1899, when arrested by Superintendent Wood and charged with murder, Mary Ansell replied: 'I am as innocent a girl as ever was born.' After the inquest and the formal committal proceedings before local magistrates Mary was eventually taken to Hertford on June 29 to stand her trial at Hertfordshire Assizes. In the wake of all the pre-trial publicity the public gallery was, inevitably, packed to the gunwales as Mary was brought up from the cells by a wardress to stand before Mr Justice Mathew and hear the charge put to her that she wilfully murdered her sister Caroline. She answered in a firm and determined voice 'Not guilty my lord'.

Outlining the case for the prosecution, Mr J.F.P. Rawlinson promised to produce evidence that would prove beyond doubt that Mary Ansell took out an insurance policy on her sister's life and then deliberately set out to kill her, firstly by putting phosphorous paste rat poison in the sugar that she had posted to Caroline and then, when that had failed, by putting much more of the same sort of poison in a cake-filling which, this time, Caroline had eaten and from which she subsequently died. He would also call evidence from a hand-writing expert which would prove that the letter purporting to have come from a cousin had, in fact, been written in a disguised hand by the defendant. The letter, said Mr Rawlinson, was of great importance to the case because Mary Ansell knew that if her sister became ill and died the asylum authorities would write to her parents and would ask for an inquiry into the case of death. So cut-and-dried was the case for the prosecution that their witnesses had completed their evidence by the middle of the afternoon of that same day.

Somewhat surprisingly, Mary's father and mother were called to give evidence against her; James Ansell recalled how his daughter had put pressure on him not to allow the asylum authorities to hold a post mortem examination on Caroline's body. Questioned by Mr W. Clarke Hall, for Mary, he agreed that his two daughters were on good terms and he had no reason to think that Mary was 'in distress' for money. Mrs Ansell said: 'The two sisters were always happy and comfortable and I never heard one say a bad word about the other.'

In the witness box Mary remained as composed as she had been in the dock. She had, she said, sent neither the cake nor the tea and sugar and not communicated with Caroline since December of 1897, some 16 months before her death. Mary admitted that she had brought some rat poison from the hardware shop but said it was for destroying vermin in the basement of the Maloney's house. Under cross-examination she was asked why, when she had bought several jars of poison only one jar, with a small amount in it, was recovered by the police. Mary replied that she had poked most of it down the rat holes with a stick and thrown the other jars away.

Asked by Mr Rawlinson why she had suddenly decided to insure her sister's life she replied; 'Because Mr Cooper pressed me to do so. I said I was fond of my sister and would like her to have a decent funeral'. Asked once again if she could truthfully say that she was fond of her sister, Mary Ansell replied: 'No two sisters who were better friends never lived!'

There was no-one else to speak on Mary's behalf except her lawyer and, although his speech to the jury was 'characterised by much earnestness' Mr Clarke Hall did little more than attempt to place an element of doubt on the prosecution's very convincing case against his client. However, if Mr Clarke Hall claimed to have exposed numerous unanswered questions in the prosecution case he and his team had made no effort to answer them themselves. No-one had traced Mary's boyfriend to discover from him how she had behaved when he had postponed their wedding; no independent doctor had been engaged to discover Mary's own mental state and no attempt had been made to discover whether there was a history of insanity in that branch of the Ansell family. Had this happened, a different verdict might have been arrived at but, as it was, the word 'guilty' was on the lips of most people before the jury had even retired.

With the verdict finally delivered Mr Justice Mathew said that it was impossible that the jury should have returned any other.

DAILY MAIL

KS OF
THE WEEK.

NEW NOVELS AND MR. MIGGS.

spondent Novelist.

F. Norris holds a place apart
among novelists. He is not disturbed
rate of the fashion of the hour.
aspires forward with eagerness to
wing fancy, but he still keeps the
if he marked out for himself in
ships. It matters not to him that
a succeeds to psychology, he is as
terested in the gyrations of M.
as in these fearsome echoes of the
man which he to-day hold the people
As he began so he will end: a
salvan to Thackeray and an author
you may lose yourself for an
hour shame and without regret.

Gentlemanly Interest.

hatever happens, he writes in the
his interest. His heroes are always
up and admirably groomed. They
on the mental demands it, and they
ing when no sport shares them to
They sip their tea in well-kept
and they make love in shrubberies
men should
all, they don't excite the reader's
and if perchance they have done
apply palliate their transgressions with
moral and wit. Therefore, we pick
and We know Mr. Norris with an assured
if takes care that we shall never be
sired.

glby.

Giles Ingilby "London Mail"
perfectly sustains its aut'
prime Ingilby is a
gentleman, whom M-
rive, whom M-
a to draw.
a hate
s

HURRYING THE EXECUTION.

MARY ANSELL'S JURORS PROTEST.

FOREMAN'S IMPRESSIVE STATEMENT.

"WE HAD NO IDEA SHE WOULD BE HANGED."

MORE EVIDENCE AS TO INSANITY.

STRIKING LETTER FROM DR. FORBES WINSLOW.

OVER TEN THOUSAND LETTERS OF PROTEST.

FURTHER RE'   ? IN PARLIAMENT.

Publi-
fort

...een lying dormant under the com-
was safe enough, has been aroused
the Home Secretary's decision

...own, over 10,000 letters of pro-
...hich so many correspondents
...e way in which the execution

...iry has been given in this

...surprised as the general
...gues, Mr. Wise, have

...he jury would have
...ged had they had
...mulated.

...da by the

"If necessary I shot
to make an affidavit t
too dreadful to thi
hanged when, knowin
she is not accountabl
"She was under :
every day, and I :
opinion that she was
hundreds of children
hands the stands
memory, simply bro
she was not right
certainly make my :
Home Secretary will

IN PAI

ANOTHER QU
HOME I

In the House of C
,noon,
Mr. Dalziel aske
with reference to tl
the case of Mary A
sisters were insane
tion was given to
sisters died in asyl
Winslow had prono
prisoner was not re
and, further, that
tion of insanity w
and whether the r
any objection to p
two experts on the
Sir M. White Ri
tice adopted by
decline to lay befo
made for the pur
giving advice to
advice I alone am
I may, however,
stances of the ca
history, have bee
sidered by me,
Winslow, who wa
by me, was befor
sidered.

LATI

A PUBLIC M
H

A corresponden
we verified by t
...porters, and who
...he incident,
...sed t

THE ANSELL SCANDAL.

HOME SECRETARY'S EXTRAORDINARY ACTION.

OVER 100 M.P.'S

D DELAY.

M.P.'S PLEA FOR DELAY.

Over 100 Members. Petition.—The
Home Secretary Curtly Refuses.

The undersigned members of the House
of Commons respectfully suggest to the Right
Hon. Sir M. White-Ridley the desirability of
postponing the execution of Mary Ansell for at
least a week to enable further inquiries to be
made into her mental condition, seeing that
a great diversity of opinion exists on the matte

THOS. BURT, Morpeth.
WILFRID LAWSON, Cockermouth.
J H. YOXALL, Gateshead.   (SIGNED)
J CARVELL WILLIAMS.
T. BAYLEY, N...

J. LOWLES, H..
W. C. STE...

Examples of the headlines provoked by the Mary Ansell case. Among the MPs petitioning the Home Secretary – a future Prime Minister, David Lloyd George.

68

It had been shown to their satisfaction that the prisoner deliberately took the life of her. sister – an afflicted woman who had never been a burden to her and who had the utmost claim upon her affection and compassion.

Throughout the pronouncements the packed court had been awaiting some visible response from Mary but she gave none. 'The condemned woman heard all this with an indifference that was almost startling' the *Daily Mail* reported the following day. 'When the foreman pronounced the one word that everyone expected, Mary Ann Ansell momentarily raised her dry unsympathetic eyes at her two sisters who were in a side gallery and then gazed fixedly at the judge. Some women almost fainted at the sight of the black cap...:but Mary did not move a muscle nor shed a single tear.' However, as the judge finished passing the death sentence with the customary phrase '...and may the Lord have mercy upon your soul,' the long chilling scream of a woman rang through the courtroom. Only then did Mary react. 'That's my mother', she cried, and was hustled to the cells below.

The campaign to gain a reprieve for Mary began almost as soon as the first newspapers were on the streets. Although everyone knew she had deliberately poisoned her sister few had believed she would be sentenced to death. Some assumed the jury would add a rider recommending mercy on the grounds that she committed the crime while the balance of her mind was disturbed; others had expected her defence counsel to produce evidence that the family had a history of insanity – but none of that happened.

Three days later, on 3rd July 1899, the *Daily Mail* fired its first shot in what was to become one of the most passionate and most sustained campaigns to stop an execution that Fleet Street has known. The paper's reporters were sent out to do the work many felt the defence solicitors should have done in the first place – namely to discover witnesses who would testify to the doomed girl's disturbed state of mind. Her former boyfriend, who was not identified by name, told the newspaper; 'Mary was very anxious to get married. She had a strong but erroneous idea that her parents were oppressing her. She bought articles of furniture early that year (1898) and told a friend she was getting married at Easter although she did not mention a single word of this to me. One day she turned up to meet me in a dress which she said was her wedding dress and when I expressed surprise she stared at me vacantly and went off and changed out of it. On another occasion she went out and rented a room to occupy when we were married, and bought things to furnish it although I had not proposed to her.' Mary's employer, Margaret Maloney, commented: 'I can truthfully say that neither my husband nor myself entertained any doubt as to Mary Ann Ansell's weak state of mind. During the time she was with me she seemed to grow decidedly worse.....:from being silly and at times vacant, as was shown by her mumbling to herself, she became positively spiteful.'

The paper also claimed to have discovered cases of insanity on both sides of the Ansell family, stating that all the mother's sisters died insane, that the father's two sisters died in an asylum and that, as well as her late sister Caroline, Mary had another younger sister who was also insane. 'If Mary Ansell is not mad,' thundered the *Mail's* leader column, 'then the laws of heredity have been almost miraculously suspended on her behalf.'

On the day the Under Sheriff for Hertfordshire announced that Mary Ansell's execution had been set for Wednesday 19th July, her solicitor, Mr Percy Wisbey of Hemel Hempstead, took the step he should have taken before the trial started. He wrote to the Home Secretary, Sir Matthew White-Ridley, and asked for permission for the condemned girl to be examined by an independent specialist. The man he chose was the country's acknowledged leading expert on lunacy, Dr Forbes Winslow. His expertise and reports had already led to new and enlightened attitudes towards mental illness and had resulted in amendments to the law affecting criminal lunacy. He had been engaged many times by the defence in criminal cases going back over 25 years and had already made an extensive study of the Ansell case. After examining the court records and reports of the way Mary had behaved before and during the trial he had already formed the opinion that she was 'a mental degenerate' and ought to be held as irresponsible in the eye of the law. 'I am of the opinion that if the question of her insanity had been raised at the trial, no jury could have convicted her upon the evidence which might

70

FRIDAY, JULY 14, 18

SHALL MARY ANSELL DIE?

A Question for the Men and Women of England to Answer.

Mary Ansell has but five days to live if the humane efforts now being made fail to induce the Home Secretary to recommend her Majesty to grant a reprieve.

In an age of culture and enlightenment the fact that a woman's life has been demanded by the law sends a thrill of shame and horror throughout the land. Only one woman—the notorious Mrs. Dwyer—has been hanged since 1895, while several have been reprieved on the ground of sex alone. But in the case of Mary Ansell it is not a matter of sentiment at all. It is a matter of right and justice—of whether a poor hapless girl shall pay the penalty of a crime, the gravity of which she was incapable of realising.

Mary Ansell is insane; of that there ~~no doubt.~~

MARY ANSELL'S
FATE.

TO BE HANGED ON WEDNESDAY MORNING.

ONE-SIDED INQUIRY.

NO BENEFIT OF THE DOUBT FOR THE PRISONER.

DR. FORBES WINSLOW'S REPORT IGNORED.

MARY ANSELL.

A courtroom sketch of Mary Ansell published by the *The Daily Mail*.

71

have been adduced. In order for a person to be legally responsible she would be supposed to know the difference between right and wrong and the nature and gravity of the act committed by her. That she did not know the difference I have not the slightest doubt. This has been confirmed by the prison chaplain – that she can't be made to understand what murder is.'

In the end, the Home Secretary did allow a re-examination of Mary's mental state – but it was a very one-sided affair. He called in the judge Mr Justice Mathew to get his views on the post-trial developments and instructed two Prison Department doctors with experience in criminal lunacy cases at Broadmoor to make a fresh examination. Despite the belated request from her solicitor Percy Wisbey, who himself signed an affidavit expressing his firm belief that she was insane, no independent doctor was allowed to examine or even represent the prisoner – Dr Forbes Winslow turned up at St Albans prison gate but was refused admission. The following day the Home Office announced that the Home Secretary 'had been unable to find any sufficient grounds to justify him in advising Her Majesty to interfere with the due course of law.' Mary would hang in four days time.

By this time the *Daily Mail's* campaign had attracted attention countrywide and on the continent as well. So when, with four days to go, the minister refused to recommend a reprieve, protests began to come in thick and fast. A remarkable development came when the foreman of the jury which convicted Mary Ansell – Charles Cusworth, of New Bushey, near Watford, – called at the *Daily Mail* offices in a state of some emotion. His object, he said, was to protest against the Home Secretary's refusal to grant a reprieve. 'I am deeply upset at seeing the decision,' he told the *Mail*. 'If her counsel had urged the plea of insanity, and put before us the evidence which has since been published, we should have been unanimous, I am sure, in recommending a commutation of the death sentence to a punishment other than a capital one.'

By now the question on half of the country's lips was: 'With such overwhelming evidence of murder against their client why on earth didn't Mary's lawyers go for the obvious defence of insanity in the first place?' The *Daily Mail* believed that it knew

72

why. It quoted another famous murder trial ten years earlier in which a wealthy Liverpool woman, Mrs Maybrick, had been sentenced to death for murdering her husband and had then been reprieved after conducting an expensive campaign to prove that she was mentally unstable at the time she committed the offence. 'The reason this course was not adopted with Mary Ansell,' the *Mail* declared, 'was that no money was forthcoming for the special inquiries necessary for evidence of imbecility. Mrs Maybrick had been able to spend vast sums on her defence....but this repulsive-looking, forlorn, imbecile and penniless servant girl had to depend upon the kindness of her lawyers to do the best they could for her without the expenditure of money'. The same day under the headline 'Shall Mary Ansell Die? the paper went overboard by producing a very crude artist's impression of Mary, accompanied by the highly emotive caption: 'Look at the photograph of the condemned girl produced herewith. Is that the face of a sane person? Is not madness pictured in every line of it? Ask any specialist in brain diseases what he thinks of a face and head of such conformation and in all likelihood he will tell you the chances are 100 to 1 that the owner is an idiot.' It could not have done their cause a lot of good.

Public opinion had lain dormant until now because most people had believed – like the jurors – that the Home Secretary would respond to the revelations about Mary's mental state and would commit her to Broadmoor. When he refused to grant a reprieve the reaction was staggering. The *Mail* alone received more than 10,000 letters and telegrams protesting against the decision to allow the execution to go ahead. All demanded clemency. On Tuesday 18th July, the eve of the execution, the matter came to a head when the Home Secretary was forced to defend his actions in Parliament.

At the same time, a lively meeting of several hundred people was taking place at The Cannon Street Hotel in the City. This had been organised by a Mr William Jobson, who had been collecting petition signatures from the start of the controversy and had already had one petition rejected by the Home Secretary. This time, Mr Jobson had assembled men and women who had already publicly voiced their disgust at the death sentence, either by writing to the newspapers or speaking out at meetings. These included members of The Metropolitan Asylums Board, and a highly influential figure in the person of The Hon. Roger Yelverton. Mr Yelverton was a prominent barrister who was Chairman of The League of Criminal Appeal. He told the company: 'If Mary Ansell is hanged then it will have to be admitted by all that there is one law for the rich and another for the poor.'

Despite Jobson's success in enlisting the support of over one hundred MPs, nothing could move the Home Secretary. With the execution just over 12 hours away, Mr Jobson and his party made one more attempt to get it delayed. They telegraphed Windsor Castle and asked Queen Victoria to receive a deputation but were told by return that they must make their representations to the Home Secretary. After one last plea they went home. It was by then nearly midnight on the eve of Mary's execution. They had done their best but could do no more.

At St Albans prison James Ansell and his wife went to see their daughter for the last time. 'The poor girl seemed quite dead within herself,' Mr Ansell told reporters waiting outside. 'She seemed quite worn out – in a sort of stupor. She just leaned against the grating helplessly. We didn't care to talk too much for fear of tormenting her. She asked me if I could forgive her and I told her that most certainly I could because if I did not forgive her I could not forgive myself.'

According to the *Herts Advertiser:* 'Mary slept comparatively well that night and, on rising at six o'clock, washed and dressed, apparently greatly refreshed as a consequence. Her last toilet completed she partook of breakfast but ate little.' The hangman Billington entered the cell just before eight o'clock. It was a brilliant sunny day and by this time there were large crowds outside the walls of St Albans prison; roads were blocked and at one point warders and policeman had to run outside to pull down a man who climbed a telegraph pole in order to get a view of the scaffold. The Gentlemen of the Press reported somewhat peevishly that they were not allowed in to witness the execution, as had been the case at the previous hanging in St Albans in 1880, but they still managed to glean sufficient details from their

74

Mary Ansell's execution at St Albans goal, – an artist's impression published in *Petit Parisien* at the time, now in the possession of The Mary Evans Picture Library.

contacts inside to publish chilling accounts of the grisly mechanics of Mary Ansell's last moments:

The gallows was no more more than 30 steps from the condemned cell...The procession was formed and a start made for the scaffold.

The condemned girl was supported on either side by a warder and on the way repeated after the Chaplain *'Oh God forgive this miserable sinner!'* On the way to the machine of death the convict appeared overcome and prayed fervently, as she walked, for help. Before she was aware of it she stood over the drop and under the gallows. Billington, who stood behind, touched her and moved her into the centre and said: "That will do. Now be brave." He then drew a cloth cap well over the woman's face, at the same time tightening the strap that was around her waist. The rope was held at the side and, stretching out his hand, he caught it and placed the noose over the woman's head, moving the steel swivel to the side of her neck. Stepping back and just as the Chaplain said *'Lord have mercy on us'* he touched the lever and Mary Ansell was launched into eternity. She fell like a log and there was not the slightest movement, the seven-foot drop making death instantaneous.'

At two minutes past eight the black flag was run up the prison flag pole where it fluttered in a light summer breeze throughout the remainder of that day. Two hours later twelve jurymen went through the prison gates to view the body and to adjudicate at the inquest. Evidence of execution was given by the Chief Warden Edward Lloyd. The formalities of the inquest over, Mary's body was placed in a coffin in quicklime and buried, by tradition, in a corner of the prison yard.

There were questions in the House afterwards but no great recriminations nor any criticism of the Home Secretary. With the battle for Mary Ansell's life lost most of the public forgot the campaign pretty quickly, their attention switching to news of the exciting prospect of British military action in a faraway land where a group of fractious Boer farmers threatened trouble at a little-known Transvaal staging post called Mafeking. However, many people in St Albans did not forget. Mary Ansell was not one of their community, nor had her terrible crime been committed in their city; but because she was brought to St Albans to be put to death they had followed the case with great concern.

The name of Mary Ansell came up on a number of occasions during the years that followed. As the public's memory of the damning evidence against her faded there was even a rumour (completely unfounded) that a brother had made a death-bed confession that it was he who had sent the poisoned cake to Caroline. St Albans prison fell into disuse after the First World War and when, in 1930, the City Council purchased the old building to use as accommodation for their Highways Department, Mary's remains, along with those of two men executed there, were re-interred in the city cemetery.

Over the years there have been suggestions that Mary's name should be included on that disturbing list of people who were hanged and later found to be innocent. Mary Ansell was certainly not 'innocent'. She carried out a carefully planned and callous murder which caused her sister to die in great agony. But in view of the large number of witnesses who were prepared to testify about the girl's unstable mental state there's little doubt that the *Daily Mail* and its supporters were right – her fellow human beings did not give her a fair trial. Phosphorous paste rat poison may make a deadly filling for a cake but in this case the combined ingredients of a schizophrenic defendant, a weak defence lawyer, a hanging judge and an obdurate Home Secretary proved to be a pretty lethal cocktail as well.

Francis Fisher of Watford, businessman, civic leader and prime target of the rioters.

The Watford Coronation Riot

★

For the loyal townspeople of Watford, as for everyone else in the British Empire, Thursday, 26th June, 1902, should have been a day of joy and celebration. It was, after all, more than sixty years since a monarch had been crowned in Westminster Abbey, and Watford like every other town and village, had been planning to mark the event with festivities on a scale never attempted before. In fact, neither event took place. On the day set aside for his coronation, King Edward VII was lying on a couch in Buckingham Palace fighting for his life and two hundred loyal citizens of Watford were fighting to protect their shops and homes from a rampaging mob of rioters who caused bloodshed and committed arson, looting, and widespread damage before they were finally quelled.

The nation had been given little warning of the Coronation crisis. Only forty-eight hours beforehand they had been stunned by the news from Buckingham Palace that King Edward had undergone a major operation for perityphlitis (appendicitis) and that the surgeons were concerned about his condition. The Coronation, of course, would have to be postponed. As it turned out the surgery performed by Sir Frederick Treves proved highly successful but since the operation was comparatively new and reckoned to carry a high degree of risk, the early bulletins on the condition of the 'illustrious patient' gave no cause for optimism. Thus, a week that had promised to be so full of good things turned into one of gloom and anxiety. The hundreds of little committees set up to organise local festivities met hurriedly to assess the situation and without exception set about cancelling their events.

At Watford the task fell upon Francis Fisher, a local butcher and businessman who was also chairman of the Town Council. He called his Coronation Committee together and all agreed that they had no option but to postpone the festivities; the children's sports in Cassiobury Park, the dinner for the aged and poor, the band concerts and procession and the lighting of the giant bonfire. Neither would it be right at this stage to give each child in the town the Coronation shilling which had been promised. Not when at any moment the nation might be mourning a dead king.

The announcement of the postponement was accepted with great disappointment but without question by most citizens, and on Wednesday the flags and bunting and other elaborate street decorations were taken down. The bonfire was left, hopefully to be lit at a later, happier, date in the summer.

The Thursday on which the Coronation should have taken place was hot and sultry. Few people bothered to go to work and crowds wandered listlessly about the town discussing the latest bulletin on the king's health but still feeling a great sense of anticlimax. As the day stretched towards evening there became apparent a feeling of unease and tension as groups of 'the rougher element' began moving through the crowds voicing more concern about their lost pleasures than for the health of their king. As they began uttering vague demands for some form of compensation, others, sensing an outlet for their disappointment, joined in. It was not long before the name of the unfortunate Councillor Francis Fisher was mentioned.

So it was that at 9.30 p.m. the elderly watchman who sat in his wooden hut guarding the bonfire witnessed with alarm a crowd of between two and three hundred people descending upon him. The ringleaders told him that since Fisher wasn't going to light his bloody bonfire, they would do it for him, and if he dared to show up, he'd end up on top of it! The huge, tinder-dry fire was blazing in a matter of moments; the old watchman was punched and bundled out of his hut which was hurled onto the fire along with the temporary fencing and other council property in the area. The town surveyor, a Mr Waterhouse, arrived to try to damp down the situation but was promptly pelted with stones. He had to take refuge in a nearby cottage which had all its windows smashed, before the mob – armed with wooden clubs, lengths of metal piping and pockets full of stones – made off towards the town centre to 'do for Fisher'.

Being in the centre of a mob during the moments building up to a full-scale riot is an uncanny experience. An angry crowd generates a tension and atmosphere of such strength that one feels one can literally reach out and touch it. The leaders and more volatile individuals move restlessly about, eyes searching for a movement, ears listening for a remark that will give them their first excuse to trigger off the violence. Such was the atmosphere in Watford High Street late that Thursday night. It was the movement of a solitary arm that set the violence under way. A stone flew through the air and the sound of breaking glass echoed down the street. A moment of silence... then, as if given a signal, the whole crowd surged forward to commit that offence which (short of treason) is the gravest form of a breach of the peace known to the English law – a riot.

The situation was one which the chief of Watford's Police Force, Superintendent Wood, was quite unable to control. Even with his full complement of some twenty men he would never have been able to contain the riot; not long before the incident began to build up, he had had to despatch half his force to Hemel Hempstead to deal with a series of minor disturbances there. So he was left with an inspector, a sergeant and a handful of mounted and foot-patrol constables. As Wood frantically telephoned neighbouring forces for more men, the mob proceeded to wreak its fury on Councillor Fisher's butcher's shop and on three other buildings, two drapery stores and a shoe shop which belonged to another member of the misunderstood Coronation Committee, Mr George Longley.

Francis Fisher had received some warning of the trouble and, with some of his staff, was attempting to barricade his premises when the rioters arrived. Although having little chance against the wall of flailing staves and metal piping they put up a stout defence for a short while, at one time slamming down the metal window shutters on the hands of several of the leading rioters who had smashed the windows and were trying to climb into the shop. The action sparked off a sensational rumour, quickly flashed through the crowd, that Fisher and his men were using meat

81

Damaged shops in Watford High Street managed to open for business the day after the riot.

cleavers to chop off people's fingers as they put them through the shutters. A rumour which in the chaos became so strong that several days after the event, some London newspapers were carrying reports that eight human fingers had been found in the sawdust on the shop floor! These reports were later strenuously denied in a statement by Mr Fisher.

In the heat of the moment, however, the rumour served to anger the rioters even more and, by sheer weight of numbers, they forced the shutters open and poured inside, forcing Mr Fisher and his men to beat a swift retreat. The leaders proceeded to pile up furniture and other materials which were then set alight, but the blaze was put out by the fire brigade before getting a hold on the building. Even then, several attempts were made to cut the firemen's hoses.

George Longley took the pillage of his premises more passively, taking no steps to defend his property, except to evacuate his wife and children. It was a shrewd move which probably saved his property from far more damage than the broken windows and fittings his three shops suffered. Instead, he chose to stand and watch as the mob proceeded to help itself to the very tempting contents. He studied the faces of the men and women very carefully as they made off with arms full of boots and shoes, rolls of calico, umbrellas, parasols, dresses, hats and hosiery. 'It was noticeable,' he said when giving evidence of identification in court later, 'that the women looters did not hurry but could be seen selecting the refinery with great care.'

By 11.30 p.m., with police reinforcements still on their way by train and horse-drawn vehicle, Superintendent Wood decided to take the only course of action left open to him; he would have to try to recruit a force of Special Constables from the townspeople to deal with the riot, which was, by then, completely out of control. His uniformed men, hopelessly outnumbered, had been attacked and knocked about quite badly. However, before the law allowed him to appeal for civilian volunteers, the Riot Act had to be read – a hazardous task assigned to the magistrate W.T. Coles, who performed it with admirable courage, standing in the Market Place and dodging the occasional lump of wood thrown from the crowd.

'Our Sovereign Lord the King chargeth and commandeth all persons being assembled immediately to disperse themselves and peaceably to depart to their habitations or to their lawful business upon the pains contained in the Act, made in the first year of King George (1714) for preventing tumultuous and riotous assemblies. GOD SAVE THE KING.'

Mr Coles' words could hardly be heard above the din – but that didn't matter; Superintendent Wood had the authority he

83

needed and when he put out his appeal for volunteers he was astonished by the response. Five hundred townsmen of all ages, who had been watching the violence with growing shame and anger, came forward. Of these, two hundred were sworn in straight away, issued with an assortment of official and improvised riot truncheons and divided into several squads, each under the command of a uniformed man. There then began a series of baton charges in which, after several bloody clashes resulting in dozens of split heads, the ringleaders were arrested and the rest of the mob finally broken up at about 3 a.m. Thirty-five people were detained that night, eight of them women, and since there was no room for them in Watford's modest police station, most were taken to St Albans gaol to await their court appearance. Perhaps the most extraordinary feature of the night was that despite the incredible amount of violence, nobody was killed or even critically injured. Inspector Boutell, a sergeant and three policemen received nasty head wounds but none was off duty for more than a few days. Several police horses were stabbed or slashed with sharp instruments, but all survived.

On the Friday morning, the people of Watford emerged to find the town centre in a state of turmoil – the street littered with broken glass, stones, lumps of wood and the occasional pool of blood. The volunteer specials, after snatching a couple of hours rest in houses opened to them by grateful residents, were out early on cleaning-up operations and, although they encountered some sporadic stoning from small groups of youths, there was no repetition of the trouble of the previous night. By this time, there had arrived on the scene the Chief Constable of Hertford-shire, Colonel Henry Daniell, and his very able lieutenant, Deputy Chief Constable John Reynolds.

If there is a legendary figure in the Hertfordshire Police Force, it is John Reynolds. A former Superintendent of the Hitchin Division he was an encyclopaedia of police experience; a rigid disciplinarian and the possessor of a fine streak of Hertfordshire cunning which kept him abreast, if not ahead of the movements of most of the county's criminals. He was an autocratic but popular law man who served the Force for the incredible period of fifty-one years. When Mr Reynolds was on the streets there was

Rioters on their way to prison. After receiving their sentences, ring-leaders of the riot were handcuffed in pairs and taken on a humiliating walk through Watford before being put into the police wagons.

never any trouble and the people of Watford saw a lot of him during the two very tense days following the riot.

He organised a merciless search of the slum hovels in Ballard's Buildings and Red Lion Yard, where most of the trouble-makers lived. The squads of specials were so thorough that by lunch-time that Friday more arrests had been made, and most of the clothing and footwear looted from Mr Longley's shops had been recovered and piled high in a room at the police station. The search became so hot that many looters panicked and surrendered their individual hauls voluntarily rather than have their homes turned upside down. While all this was going on, Reynolds had taken the precaution of employing the services of a number of carpenters in the town, who spent the day busy at their lathes, turning out dozens of new truncheons!

85

Mr George Longley at the door of one of three shops belonging to him which were looted by the rioters.

Later in the day, a strange procession made its way along Watford High Street past the damaged shops to the police court. A horse bus, a wagonette and several tradesmen's carts borrowed for the occasion and each with a couple of policemen aboard, were flanked by more mounted police as the prisoners were brought back from St Albans gaol to appear before a special court. Ironically, only a small number of townspeople were there to witness this procession since most had gone to the railway station, thinking the prisoners would be brought in by train. Fortunately for them, none of the prisoners was charged with offences under the Riot Act, which carried maximum penalties of penal servitude for life. The charges, instead, were confined to assault, larceny and attempted arson. At this and subsequent court hearings forty-six men and eight women were found guilty and received sentences ranging from fines or fourteen days' imprisonment to ten months' hard labour.

On the day when most of the heavier prison sentences were handed out, Deputy Chief Constable Reynolds took the ringleaders on a final humiliating walk through part of the town before putting them into the wagons that carried them off to prison. Handcuffed in pairs and surrounded by a strong force of policemen, they were marched past lines of silent townsfolk. A reporter for the *Watford Observer* watched their journey. 'As they left, they affected an air of bravado,' he wrote. 'But when the last house passed them, their faces changed and more than one was seen to be crying.'

Because the Riot Act had been read, all the victims received full compensation from Town Hall funds, a bill which came to more than £2,000. The two hundred special constables were each given their riot truncheons as a souvenir of the occasion. King Edward got better and on the day of his delayed Coronation the Watford festivities went ahead much as originally planned. It was, however, some years before the town was able to live down the unique and unflattering headlines which it earned during the crisis of King Edward's illness.

Railway Disaster!

★

The astonishing disclosures of negligence made after the Hitchin to Royston train disaster in 1866 were more than enough to provoke a national scandal. The fact that the event was accepted as little more than 'an unfortunate accident' reveals a good deal about the extraordinary lack of concern shown by Victorian travellers over the hair-raising incidents that were occurring almost daily on their railways.

The train was the morning express from King's Cross to Cambridge. When it pulled out of Hitchin station at 10.20 a.m. on 3rd July it was running only a minute or two late. In the second class carriages immediately behind the engine were groups of workmen, some employed by the Great Northern Railway Company, others on their way to put up telegraph lines. In the two first class carriages which followed were a few passengers destined mainly for Royston and Cambridge. The first ten miles of the journey were uneventful; the train stopped at Ashwell and then trundled on along the Hertfordshire border towards Royston.

About two miles from the town, when it was approaching the Litlington level crossing the train, according to passengers' statements later, was 'travelling at its normal speed of about 30 miles an hour'. Suddenly, the engine lurched violently to the left and jumped the rails; it careered along the track for eighty yards and then rolled down the embankment, turning over twice before coming to rest on its wheels in a field of barley. Although the coupling between the engine and the second class carriages broke away, the jolt was severe enough to throw them off the track as well and they also overturned, trapping the workmen inside. The impact on the first class carriages was rather less and, although derailed, they stayed upright.

Arthur Nash, a lawyer from Royston, was in one of these carriages and, with several fellow passengers, he jumped out on

88

Sightseers and railway staff with the wrecked engine and brake van after it had been brought back to Hitchin.

to the track and ran to give help. He found the engine driver, Andrew Hunter, aged 25, and his stoker William Clark, aged 31, lying in the field both dying from fearful head injuries. Realising there was nothing they could do to help the crew, Nash and the others set to work to free the nine workmen, still trapped in the crushed remains of the second class carriage. They managed to release all the men who, although seriously injured, survived their ordeal. Having seen the casualties away to hospital, Arthur Nash turned his attention to the railway track and his findings formed an important part of the evidence at the inquest on the dead railwaymen.

'I examined the track,' he said, 'and some of the sleepers were very rotton indeed. I saw men kick the rotton wood away.' Other early indications of the appalling state of this section of the line were given by the widows of the dead train crew. Mrs Ellen Hunter recalled: 'My husband had remarked many times how tired he was after travelling over this stretch of line, from having been shaken about so much.' The stoker's widow, Hannah Clarke, told the coroner that her husband had declared on several occasions that it was not safe to travel on that section of the track.

Hitchin railway station in the 1870s.

The inquest was then adjourned for an official Board of Trade investigation by Captain W.H. Tyler of the Royal Engineers and when his report was presented several days later, the evidence of earlier witnesses was more than confirmed.

'Looking from the point of the accident towards Hitchin,' the Captain reported, 'one could see the rails were in a wavy condition for a distance of 220 yards.' It was not difficult for him to explain this condition either, since not only were most of the wooden sleepers 'in the last stages of rottenness' – but also there were only half as many under each section of rail as there should have been! Nor were the rails properly fitted; they were sitting in loose clamps which had been fixed to the sleepers with an assortment of spikes and nails. There were not even any 'fish-plates', those essential standard fittings used to bolt the end of each section of rail to the next! Not unnaturally, the constant pounding of suc-

90

cessive trains on the loose rail ends had caused numerous chips in the rails themselves.

The Captain also made a thorough inspection of the ill-fated engine after it had been taken back to the sheds at Hitchin. It was, he discovered, a single-tank engine of a kind which should never have been used to pull a passenger train since – because of its weight and design – it would have run less steadily, particularly on such a bad track as the one between Hitchin and Royston. Captain Tyler also discovered that one of the main suspension springs in the engine had been fractured for a considerable time before the accident and this had apparently gone unnoticed the last time it was serviced. So he deduced that the bad state of the track and the unsteadiness of the engine with the fractured spring had combined to cause it to jump the rails with disastrous results.

Having decided how the accident was caused, Captain Tyler went on to interview the senior engineers of both the Great Northern and Great Eastern Railway Companies to try to establish how it was that the track had reached this state of neglect. It turned out that until 1st April 1866 (eight weeks before the accident), the line had belonged to the Great Eastern Railway Company, and their engineer had examined it in December 1865 and had ordered 11,400 new sleepers to be inserted in the permanent way. Clearly, he wasn't worried by a sense of urgency, since when the Great Northern acquired the line four months later none of the work had been done, and the 11,400 sleepers were handed over to the succeeding company for them to put in. Great Northern's engineer appears to have regarded the need for track repairs as rather more urgent and workmen began laying the new sleepers almost straight away. By July, of the eighteen miles of double track ear-marked for repair, eleven had been completed, but that unfortunately did not include the worst section near the Litlington level crossing.

However, Captain Tyler's report concluded on a note of reassurance. 'I am glad to learn,' he wrote, 'that in addition to the greatly increased force of men which was employed after the line was taken over in April, the numbers have been still further augmented so that the re-laying of the whole eighteen miles may be completed in twelve weeks. The joints of the rails and the fastenings should in the meantime be very carefully attended to. Orders have wisely been given to slacken the speed of trains, pending the completion of this re-laying; and posts have been erected and wires strained for providing telegraphic communications which, strange to say, had not previously been supplied.'

What then, following these disturbing disclosures, did the coroner and jury have to say? In short, very little. There were no public reprimands for Great Northern for failing to impose a strict speed limit earlier on a section of track they must have known was highly dangerous; there was no criticism, beyond Captain Tyler's mild rebukes, about the use of a badly maintained and incorrect engine to haul a passenger train. Incredibly, nobody seems to have seen fit to publicly condemn the appalling track maintenance record of the Great Eastern Company who, in the fourteen years during which they had been responsible for the line, had allowed it to deteriorate to a point of total collapse and even then had done nothing positive about it. Neither was this the first crash on their section of the Cambridge branch line. Only a month earlier there had been another serious derailment between Royston and Cambridge. At the enquiry into the earlier incident the engine driver (having been lucky enough to escape with his life) told another Board of Trade inspector that he had complained to a superior about the weakness and danger of the track, but nothing had been done.

The jury at Royston, meanwhile, were unanimous in returning a verdict of accidental death on the crew of the tank engine, echoing Captain Tyler's remarks that, as the line was unsafe, it would be 'imprudent' to run trains at such a high rate of speed. Far from wishing to offer any criticism of the railway companies they chose instead to 'highly commend' the Great Northern Railway for the improvements they were making, which they were sure would eventually make the line 'one of the soundest in the kingdom.'

By Victorian standards the outcome of the Hitchin to Royston train disaster was not unusual and the men of the district who adjudicated at the enquiry were merely reflecting a nationwide attitude that was prevalent at the time. In 1866, the railways were still developing and were regarded as a new and exciting

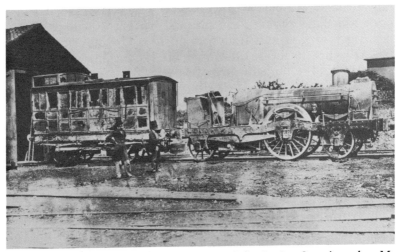

Captain Tyler, the accident investigator and the Station Superintendent Mr J Marmaduke Constable.

means of transport. The rival railway companies having invested vast sums of money in laying ten thousand miles of track were concered not so much with safety but with getting better returns from faster and more efficient services. Because it was still too early for a national code of safety to have been developed, each company had its own standards which, only painful experience was to prove, were completely inadequate. It seems unbelievable, for example, that these companies were running trains capable of 60 miles an hour with no brakes beyond a primitive wooden block system on the engine wheels, operated by hand! This, coupled with highly unreliable signalling systems, set a predictable course for rail disasters, which happened with horrifying regularity.

In 1866, Captain Tyler and three colleagues from the Board of Trade investigated no fewer than eighty major rail accidents in the United Kingdom, many far worse than the Hitchin to Royston disaster. There were two more in Hertfordshire that same year. On 9th June, three goods trains were involved in a collision inside Welwyn tunnel, resulting in the deaths of two

93

railwaymen and injury to two others. A neglectful guard and a poor signalling system were blamed. On 11th October twelve passengers sitting in a stationary train at Hitchin station were injured when a goods train, mercifully travelling at under 10 miles an hour, rammed it from behind. The driver of the goods train was fined.

Contemporary accounts of these disasters show that public concern for better safety standards was only temporarily aroused if members of the public were themselves actually killed or maimed. The deaths of railwaymen were regarded as rather more inevitable. Reports of accidents frequently made the point – not 'unfortunately the crew was killed' but 'fortunately *only* the crew was killed'. This casual approach to the high mortality rate among railwaymen was a point taken up with some force by the editor of *Railway Gazette* in the Christmas issue in 1866.

After dutifully listing the progress and profits of the various railway companies the editor went on to reveal some statistics which they, no doubt, would have preferred to have left buried. The previous year the companies had paid out more than £330,000 in compensation to some of the victims of railway disasters or their dependants. In all, 221 people had died and 1,132 had been injured – and of the dead more than half were railwaymen. 'The companies,' the editor wrote, 'are not compelled by law to send a note of such trifles to the Board of Trade (on the principle we presume that they are entitled to do what they like with their own) and it may be safely concluded that this list is very far from complete. The causes of all this slaughter and maiming demand a separate investigation.'

It was, however, many years before the Board of Trade was able to pressure the powerful railway chiefs to think as much about safety regulations as they did about profits. Although these men were often guilty of negligence, it was not always deliberate negligence. The regulations may have been primitive but they were made, for the most part, by men with a high sense of responsibility. Their failures were, more often than not, caused simply by a lack of experience. A frequent remark heard from train drivers and engineers at Board of Trade enquiries or inquests was 'I never believed it could have happened'. Time after time, events proved that it could. Most railway companies were prepared to accept the findings and recommendations which came out of these enquiries; the trouble was, that advice came too late to benefit the victims at whose inquest it was given.

Andrew Hunter and William Clarke were just two out of hundreds who died before the autocratic Victorian pioneers of Britain's railways finally acknowledged that power and speed were no good without the equipment and regulations to control them.

Arthur Melbourne-Cooper.

The Film Pioneer
of St Albans

★

On a summer afternoon in 1906 the villagers of Shenley in Hertfordshire were startled out of their wits by the sight of a machine which, so far as Edwardian England was concerned, belonged only to the science-fiction world of H. G. Wells. The sleek lines resembled those of a modern racing car and the grey armour-plated body was surmounted by a rotating turret from which protruded two sinister machine guns. As it clattered to a halt in a cloud of dust, a flap at the front opened, and out scrambled a crowd of noisy and very frightened chickens.

In time, the people living in the country areas between Barnet and St Albans became used to such happenings and, for the most part, came to regard them with amusement; none realised that what they were witnessing was the work of a remarkable pioneer of the British Cinema Industry, a man who in many ways was years ahead of his time, but whose naivety in what, even then, was a hard business world, caused him to become one of the cinema's forgotten men.

Arthur Melbourne-Cooper was born at St Albans in 1874, the son of the city's first and most successful portrait photographer, Thomas Melbourne-Cooper. As a boy he learned the art of photography from his father the hard way, spending many hours a week coating glass plates with emulsion or printing orders in the dark room while his friends were out at play. It was an unofficial apprenticeship which paid off, for by the time he was 18, young Melbourne-Cooper was an accomplished still photographer, ready to embark on a career which even in Victorian times, was considered a very respectable profession. It was with this background that, in 1892, he applied for a job as assistant to a Barnet man, Birt Acres, who at this time was reaching an exciting

97

stage in experiments with a camera he had designed to take moving pictures. As with the men who developed the art of still photography some fifty years earlier, there is controversy even today over precisely who should be accredited with which invention – though it is fair to say that Acres was at this time working almost in parallel with the more celebrated pioneers of motion pictures, Thomas Edison in America and the Lumiere brothers in France and, as such, can be described as one of the early pioneers of the British cinema. In fact, the practical development of the motion picture in Britain is dated from the granting of a patent to Acres in May 1895 for a combined cine-camera and projector with appliance for loop-forming. He had worked on this equipment with Robert Paul, a Hatton Garden optical-instrument maker, who later claimed that the country's very first film presentation using this equipment took place in his workshop. It was a claim which provoked a whole series of arguments and acrimonious debates.

However, throughout this time Arthur Melbourne-Cooper was working as Birt Acres' assistant, operating the new equipment on a series of assignments around the country. In 1895 they filmed the Derby, the Boat Race and the Henley Royal Regatta, becoming the first newsreel men to record people and scenes from everyday life. At the end of the year they assembled a collection of their films and on 14th January, 1896, gave what is now the first *recorded* public screening of motion pictures in Britain – before members of the Royal Photographic Society in London. In the same year, Acres took their films and his Kineopticon, as he called it, to Marlborough House where a dinner party was being held to celebrate the approaching wedding of Princess Maud and Prince Charles of Denmark. The show, commanded by the Prince of Wales (later King Edward VII), was seen by more than forty crowned heads of Europe and can be described as the first Royal Command Film Performance.

In fact, film shows during this period were not just the prerogative of photographic experts and royalty. Many ordinary men and women in Hertfordshire were given unexpected previews during 1895-96 as Acres and Melbourne-Cooper sought to try out the Kineopticon on a live audience in preparation for the more important viewings later on. One such event was held in Barnet Town Hall and included film of the Barnet Militia on parade in the town. For this epic, Melbourne-Cooper was deputed to stand behind the screen and add sound effects by blowing a bugle! Melbourne-Cooper himself claims to have given a show at Welham Green Boys School, North Mimms during Christmas 1895, when villagers saw a series of local scenes and comedy episodes performed for the cameraman by some of the more extrovert locals. One – *A Study in Black and White* – showed a man throwing flour over another, who retaliated by throwing soot.

In these very early days none of the films shown was longer than fifty feet and each lasted only a couple of minutes. The conditions under which they were shown were sufficient to chill the heart of any present-day fire safety officer. The fire risk involved must have been substantial as excited villagers crowded into their tiny hall, packed around the projector and its highly-inflammable film – a projector lit, not by electricity but by a very bright gas jet supplied by gas from a pressure bag on the floor nearby. It was quite a common occurrence as the performance wore on and the gas light began to dim, for Melbourne-Cooper to brighten the picture by getting a number of small boys to sit on the gas bag to squeeze the last ounce of gas towards the burning jet.

Melbourne-Cooper and Birt Acres were men of very different personalities. Acres was a scientist, an inventor whose interest in the new medium was much more academic than commercial. Melbourne-Cooper, on the other hand, was an artist with a natural sense of humour who, even at this time, saw a great future for motion pictures as a source of entertainment and towards the end of the century he began freelance camera work for some of the handful of pioneer film companies which were beginning to get established in London. He claimed to be the first man in Britain to make an advertising film when, in 1897, he shot a film for Bird's Custard Powder. It was simple and, as with most of his work, contained a degree of humour. It showed a contemporary Bird's poster coming to life; an old man walked downstairs carrying a tray of eggs. Predictably, he tripped over, smashing

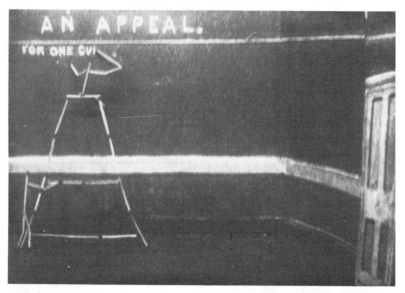

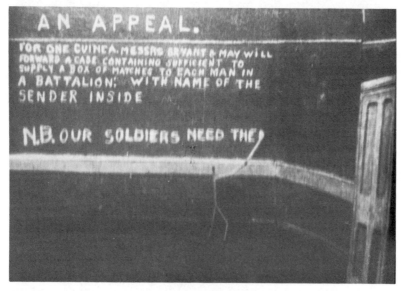

Two clips from the oldest surviving British advertising film made for Bryant and May's Matches during the Boer War.

them. The message was that he had no cause to worry because – he used Bird's Custard Powder. Two years later he made what is believed to be the earliest surviving British advertising film, sponsored by Bryant and May and taking the form of an appeal to the public to buy matches to send to troops fighting in the Boer War.

It was for this film that he used a technique for which he is now acknowledged as a pioneer – animation – or the use of a series of single-frame exposures of models to create a sequence of moving pictures. He made a box of Bryant and May matches open up and the contents pop out one at a time and march like soldiers to form a ladder to a blackboard where one 'wrote' the message:

> 'For one guinea Messrs Bryant and May will forward a case containing sufficient to supply a box of matches to each man in a battalion: with the name of the sender inside.'

Up to 1900 there were few places of entertainment prepared to show films regularly. The Music Hall managers called them 'chasers-out' because they found audiences leaving after the live show, apparently not interested in the films. A few London theatres staged performances of films showing important events but, for the most part, these now-priceless records of late Victorian life had only one regular outlet – the fairgrounds, where the more enterprising showmen saw them as a bigger money-spinner than the traditional peepshows which normally occupied so many fairground booths. Melbourne-Cooper once recalled that he received no basic fee for making an advertisement film, only £1 from the sponsors for every copy he could get shown at a fairground.

It was because of his determination to lift the film industry from this lowly status of fairground booths that he decided in 1901 to set up his own film-making company in his home town of St Albans, with a long-term plan to establish a cinema there as a place of entertainment in its own right. He formed a company called Alpha Cinematograph Films and launched himself into a career which was astonishing not only for its introduction of new camera techniques but also for its prolific output. In a matter of a year or two, Arthur Melbourne-Cooper became a figure known and respected throughout the industry; a founder-member of the Kinematograph Manufacturers' Association he found his services in almost daily demand.

He derived enormous benefit from an episode in 1903 when he was commissioned by the Duke of Devonshire to go to Chatsworth House, in Derbyshire, to film a garden party given for King Edward VII and Queen Alexandra. He astonished the guests by developing the film and showing it in the ballroom the same evening. 'A record in such matters in connection with a private house', the Court Correspondent of the *Daily Telegraph* reported the following morning. Later the same year he persuaded the London and North-Western Railway to allow him to convert a coach into a dark room and went up to Liverpool to film the Grand National. By processing the film in the coach on the way back to London he was able to show it to an audience at the Empire Theatre, Leicester Square, at 10.45 p.m. the same evening.

In 1904 he made a drama called *Rescue in Mid-Air* using actors and puppets and achieved a sequence (emulated many years later in *Mary Poppins*) in which a young nursemaid, stranded up a church tower, floated to safety with the help of an umbrella. He pioneered hilarious screen chases, using motor cars, clowns and comic policemen some years before the arrival of that classic American film comedy team the Keystone Cops. He even made a horror film, *Resurrection of Rameses,* in which an Egyptian mummy came to life and terrorised the local inhabitants – but the distributors considered it too horrific and he was unable to sell it either in Britain or America.

His film *The Motor Pirate,* of which clips still survive, is now generally regarded as one of his masterpieces. He constructed around his own car the futuristic tank which alarmed the residents of Shenley and thereabouts so much, and devised the story of a mechanised monster which rumbled through the countryside devouring all that came within its path. To obtain this effect, chickens were put into a crate in the front of the vehicle and then

A frame from *The Motor Pirate* (1906) showing the futuristic space car which Melbourne-Cooper constructed over his own vehicle.

filmed as the hatch opened and they scrambled out. The operation was repeated with a policeman tumbling out of the front. However, the camera used to take these pictures was upside down, so that when the film was processed and added to the rest of the film back-to-front, the audience saw the sequence in reverse, with chickens and policeman being apparently sucked into the machine.

By this time, Alpha Studios were producing almost a film a day including documentaries on fishing boats and the Royal Mint, short comedies, animated cartoons, almost everything upon which the cinema industry of today is based. His *Dream of Toyland*, employing dolls, toy animals, miniature cars and buses in a street set built in his studios, sold well over three hundred copies, including more than seventy to America. By 1908 his business was earning a lot of money and he was able to fulfil the

103

final part of his early ambitions. The studio property which he rented in Alma Road extended over two acres and it was here that he converted an old Polytechnic building into the Alpha Picture Palace – the first British picture palace to have a sloping floor and separate projection booth, and also the first to depart from the standard theatre practice of charging more for the seats at the front than for those at the rear. It was an innovation which attracted comment in the industry's leading trade magazine *The Bioscope:*

> 'It is a feature worthy of note,' wrote the visitor, 'that the lower priced places are in front and the better ones at the back. This arrangement was somewhat resented at first by the patrons of the higher priced seats, but when they found that the specially-raised floor gave them a better view than could be got from the front, they appreciated the innovation. The operator's box does not stand in the usual place inside the auditorium. It is a roomy apartment built out as an annex, and therefore affords immunity from accident as well as from interference from the public.'

Alpha Studies were, by this time, working flat out, seven days a week. Melbourne-Cooper who, up to now, had not only filmed but acted in many of his productions, was obliged to concentrate on the business side and employ more technicians, authors and professional actors on a regular basis. Men and women working on the West End stage would take an early morning train out to St Albans to spend several hours acting in the quaint silent dramas and comedies at the studios. Many were performed on a revolving set which Melbourne-Cooper had designed so that it could be turned to face the sun as the day progressed. Other scenes, including many chase-sequences, were shot in the streets of St Albans itself, the actresses having to put up with a barrage of ribald remarks from crowds of young lads gathered to watch the filming. Some of these often had to be ejected forcibly from the set as they tried to get in on the act. A full-length film, of around five hundred feet, would be completed in a couple of days, despite the distractions and the problems caused by the capricious weather. Many actors jumped at the chance to take part – they welcomed the change from stage performances and the pay (7s 6d. a day, with railway fare and lunch thrown in) was considered very handsome.

The year that Arthur Melbourne-Cooper opened the Alpha Picture Palace was also the year that the cinema, as we know it today, really arrived in Britain – despite the popular theory that it was not until the First World War that it became a socially-acceptable form of entertainment. It had achieved the status of a major industry well before the end of the Edwardian era. From 1908 onwards there was a burst of activity in towns and cities throughout the South, the Midlands and the North as old public halls, variety theatres, shops and even warehouses were hastily converted into picture palaces. By 1912 there were four thousand in the British Isles, though few were of the high quality of the St Albans cinema. Many were small with only narrow benches for seating and the absolute minimum of decoration and comfort. Melbourne-Cooper's had quite exotic decor, coloured electric arc-lighting and a refreshment lounge. Nevertheless, whatever standards they offered, each was an outlet for all the popular films of the day, thus contributing to the growth of the industry.

If 1908-09 was the year of the growth of the British cinema, it was also the year that marked the beginning of the decline of Arthur Melbourne-Cooper's distinguished career. That decline was signalled by his opening a second Picture Palace in Letchworth Garden City, the dream town of Sir Ebenezer Howard, where the arrival of such a frivolous institution was far from welcome. During his negotiations to rent a property in the town Melbourne-Cooper received a curt note from one council official telling him that neither his picture palace nor his noisy car was welcome in the Garden City! He persevered, though, giving a number of free performances in an effort to win over the local population, and the Letchworth Picture Palace opened in 1909, but it never made any money for Melbourne-Cooper.

From that point on, the St Albans cinema pioneer went deeper and deeper into troubled financial waters. He owned none of the properties from which he ran his studios and cinemas and, as his debts mounted, the crisis point was reached in 1911 when he, his wife and two small daughters were evicted by court bailiffs

Chase sequence from an early comedy film, shot in Upper Latimer Road, St Albans, with Melbourne-Cooper playing the postman.

from their house, and all their personal effects seized – all, that is, except for a small amount of family silver which Melbourne-Cooper's wife, Kate, smuggled out in bags concealed beneath her petticoat. During the next three years the family lived in the London area; Melbourne-Cooper found work and made one more attempt to establish an independent film-making and exhibition company. It had its head office in Warwick Court, Holborn, and when it, too, ran into debt and the rates on the property fell into serious arrears, Arthur Melbourne-Cooper was taken to court and sentenced to a month in Brixton Prison. It was an undignified exit and a rather unjust ending to a career which had contributed so much to the growth of the British cinema for, from that point on, Melbourne-Cooper and his reputation began to slip from public memory.

At first, it may be difficult to imagine how this could happen in view of the staggering output of the Alpha Studios during the preceding decade. It would seem that Melbourne-Cooper's films, at least, should have kept his name before the public eye. The trouble was that his business aptitude was so lacking that he didn't think of establishing any form of copyright on his productions. He sent them off to the distributors and agents unmarked, leaving the more astute among them to add their own trademarks later on. As a result many of the miniature masterpieces which Arthur Melbourne-Cooper created were credited to other people in later years.

There is little doubt, too, that his downfall can be attributed partly to the social atitudes of the time. Consider the impact which the opening of a film studio would have on a small, close-knit Edwardian community such as St Albans. Here was the son of their most respected portrait photographer suddenly bringing into their midst a circus of people who one normally associated only with the suspect 'gay life' of the big cities. London actresses – nicknamed, unfairly by some 'The Alpha Harem' – cavorting about the streets of a cathedral city, making films for the hoi-polloi of the fairgrounds! Nobody actually voiced any criticism in public but the disapproval was there, beneath the surface. This suspicion of moving pictures and the tales they told is well illustrated by an episode which occurred in a local Congregational Church Hall, to which Melbourne-Cooper had been invited to present a show. He took with him a fairly standard selection of one-reelers which included one entitled *What the Farmer Saw*. This was a piece of the mildest Edwardian titillation, in which a farmer, looking through a telescope, sees a young couple out on a bicycle ride. The young lady appears in some distress as a button on her boot has become undone. Her beau gallantly bends down to help and there is a close-up view of the lady's booted ankle. That was all – but when the film reached this point on the night it was shown in the Congregational Hall, the performance was ended abruptly. The local lay preacher worried lest his flock should be corrupted, had jumped up and hastily hung his cap over the lens of the projector!

The motion picture is the only truly new art form to emerge this century. Melbourne-Cooper was something of a visionary whose creative mind had been quick to exploit it as a means of communication and entertainment, in the certainty that one day it would become accepted as a part of everyday life. Like so many artists who have tried to place something new and rather re-volutionary before a cautious public he was treated with a certain amount of suspicion and gentle contempt; regarded as an eccentric who was dabbling in some brief technical gimmickry in which even the fairground masses would lose interest one day. Consequently, when his lack of business experience landed him in trouble, he was offered sympathy but no practical help.

His family believe that he was finally bowled over by his own enthusiasm, in that he tried to do too many things. Had he confined himself simply to making films his independent career might have survived, instead of ending in humiliation in the cells of Brixton Prison.

With the outbreak of the First World War, Arthur Melbourne-Cooper announced that he was going to France as a newsreel cameraman, but bowed to the pleas of his wife to put his home and family first; instead, he spent the war years inspecting shells at a munitions factory in Luton. Later he took his family to Southend, where he spent a few years working as a still photographer, and then moved North to spend the rest of his working life making advertising films for a Blackpool company. He retired to the village of Coton, near Cambridge, just before the Second World War, and died in 1961 at the age of 87.

Arthur Melbourne-Cooper did not die in complete obscurity. In the 1950s his daughter Audrey (a baby in the year the family was evicted from its home in St Albans) began what turned out to be a twenty-year quest to find the evidence that would convince historians that her father's name should be included among the pioneers of the British film industry; searching for clips of his early films, discovering old documents and records in newspaper and museum archives. A short while before her father's death she had discovered sufficient material to mount an exhibition in St Albans, held, appropriately, in the foyer of the Odeon Cinema which now stands on the site of the old Alpha Studios. Arthur Melbourne-Cooper returned briefly to the limelight as a guest-of-honour.

It is only since his death that much more evidence has come to light with the result that film historians and reference books are beginning, at last, to include the name of Melbourne-Cooper in their list of British cinema pioneers – acknowledging in particular his work on animation and his development of the cinema as a place of entertainment in its own right.

The Aviators

★

Captain Patrick Hamilton took his fragile wooden flying machine into the air from a field near Wallingford in Berkshire shortly after 0600 hours on a gusty September morning in 1912. Flying conditions were not ideal but they were not the worst the aviator had encountered. Captain Hamilton was not alone; sitting muffled up in the wicker seat in front of him was Lieutenant Atholl Wyness-Stuart, his observer, and in a second aircraft just behind, was Hamilton's flight commander, Major Brooke Popham. Three Army officers who, fascinated by the exciting prospects of powered flight, had left their regiments to join the fledgling ranks of the Royal Flying Corps.

Neither pilot had held a licence for much more than a year and Hamilton had already had a narrow escape from death while flying in America, when his aircraft crashed after being sucked into an air pocket. In fact, the three men were flying at a time when there was still much to be learned about aviation and when many still held doubts about its potential. Since there was as yet no aeronautical language, motoring terms were frequently applied to these new vehicles of the air. The control column was 'the steering wheel', the metal engine casing or cowling was 'the bonnet' and airfields were known, daintily, as 'alighting grounds'. The aviators had no standard flying kit beyond an assortment of leather coats and jerkins, breeches and leather caps which had been designed originally for the pioneer motorists and motor-cyclists. Nevertheless, on that Friday morning of 6th September 1912, the three men were on an important military mission, the outcome of which was awaited with great interest by the generals in Whitehall.

Although it was not until the 1914-18 war that these early aircraft were developed into proper fighting machines, the War Office had recognised their possible usefulness as a means of

The Daily Mirror

THE MORNING JOURNAL WITH THE SECOND LARGEST NET SALE.

No. 2,769. SATURDAY, SEPTEMBER 7, 1912 One Halfpenny.

TERRIBLE AIR FATALITY AT THE MANŒUVRES: TWO BRITISH OFFICERS DASHED TO DEATH NEAR HITCHIN YESTERDAY.

A deep shadow has been cast over the opening of the Army manœuvres by an aeroplane disaster which occurred at the village of Graveley, near Hitchin, yesterday. While flying in rough weather, the Army aeroplane No. 258 was caught in a gale and wrecked, the two occupants—Captain Hamilton, the pilot, and Lieutenant Wyness-Stuart, the observer—being instantly killed. When the machine crashed to the earth it fell into a hedge. The front portion of the machine, a monoplane, was buried in the hedge, while the engine was found lying in an adjoining field. The large photograph shows how the machine was smashed to matchwood. The small ones show Captain Hamilton (who is wearing a white sweater) and Lieutenant Wyness-Stuart.—(*Daily Mirror* photographs.)

The Graveley air disaster – the first in which airmen were killed flying on active service – was a major news story throughout much of the Western world.

aerial observation, replacing the balloons and baskets and man-lifting kites used during the Boer War. Preliminary trials on Salisbury Plain a few weeks earlier had proved that aircraft could be used to great advantage to spot enemy positions and troop movements and to drop messages to their own troops in the forward lines. Now the time had come to test these 'air scouts' and their flying machines in a large-scale battle situation. This was the mission of the three aviators as their little aircraft set off on a north-easterly course for the fifty-mile flight to North Hertfordshire and the war games.

The Army manoeuvres taking place in eastern England that autumn had been organised on an impressive scale. There were 75,000 regular soldiers and reservists taking part in a mock battle in which Blue Force was defending London against the Red Force invaders who had landed on the east coast. Captain Hamilton and Major Brooke Popham were on reconnaissance for the defenders. As their aircraft reached the Hertfordshire border the three men waved and Brooke Popham in his faster bi-plane broke away to make for his own reconnaissance area. That moment was the last time he saw his two colleagues alive. When he touched down at the R.F.C. rendezvous point at Willian, near Hitchin later that morning, he learned that Captain Hamilton and Lieutenant Wyness-Stuart were lying dead beneath the wreckage of their aircraft, barely a mile away.

To the people of North Hertfordshire, flying machines were still very much a cause of wonder and excitement; when one passed overhead, which was rarely, work stopped, housewives ran to their windows and small boys jumped on their bicycles to pedal off furiously in vain pursuit. Consequently, when Captain Hamilton brought his Deperdussin monoplane over Stevenage and began his descent over the villages towards the Willian alighting ground, hundreds of eyes were upon him. There were many, therefore, who witnessed with horror the deaths of the two men. Because there were so many witnesses it was some time before a full and accurate picture of the last moments of the Deperdussin and its crew was completed.

Nearly all estimated that the aircraft was at about six hundred feet when the trouble began. Some claimed to have seen one of the aviators fall from the aircraft to his death some time before

111

AFTER YESTERDAY'S AERIAL TRAGEDY: ARMY MONOPLANE, WHICH WON A £2,000 PRIZE, REDUCED TO MATCHWOOD.

Captain Patrick Hamilton 'at the wheel' of the Deperdussin with a French Army visitor during manoeuvres on Salisbury Plain a week before the disaster.

the machine began its final dive. One said it 'plummeted to earth like a dart', another that it 'fluttered to the ground like a bird shot on the wing'. However, most agreed that the 100 horse power Gnome engine, capable of producing speeds of 70 knots, was giving the pilot trouble well before the crash dive. It was clear, too, that – for some reason – the port wing folded and collapsed while the pilot, his engine having cut out, was desperately trying to reduce height for an emergency landing at Willian. Instead, his aircraft virtually disintegrated in mid-air and fell several hundred feet to plunge into a thick hedge at the bottom of a meadow belonging to Mr Walter Brett, landlord of the *George and Dragon* public house at Graveley. 'I saw the aircraft wobbling about,' Mr Brett was to tell the coroner later. 'It dipped and then came a report like a gun. Then the aircraft seemed to collapse altogether. I was too horrified to look any more... I ran down and found the officers lying with the machine on top of them.' Both had died immediately upon impact.

While villagers and servicemen were working to remove the bodies from the wreckage, news of the sensational crash spread like wildfire. Sightseers came from miles around, lured by the fascinating horror of this new kind of disaster. They saw the shrouded bodies carried to the horse-drawn ambulance that conveyed them to a mortuary next to St Saviour's Church in Hitchin. Some began searching the crash area and making off with pieces of the wreckage as souvenirs; the steering wheel of the Deperdussin eventually vanished this way and the curio-hunters almost prevented the investigators from discovering the cause of the crash – almost, but not quite.

Fortunately it was an official who found the small length of connecting rod, fractured at both ends, lying two hundred yards from where most of the Deperdussin had fallen. Thus, at the inquest, Hamilton's flight commander and the works manager of British Deperdussin were between them able to supply enough evidence for the jury to be satisfied that it was a mechanical fault and not pilot error or bad flying conditions that had caused the crash. Speculation before the inquest had suggested that with the wind that day gusting up to 40 knots, it had been too dangerous for the aviators and that they should never have taken off; but Major Brooke Popham said both Captain Hamilton and his aircraft had flown safely in far worse conditions than had existed that Friday.

Both he and Mr Fritz Koolhoven, of British Deperdussin, agreed that the cause of the crash was the fracture of the connecting rod, used to operate the exhaust valves of the engine. Having broken away, the rod thrashed about inside for several minutes eventually causing a large section of the engine bonnet to break away; this, in turn, flew back, cutting through one of the main wire struts supporting the port wing. The wing then began to vibrate violently and it was only a matter of minutes before the wooden structure folded and collapsed completely. 'After such a breakage,' Mr Koolhoven commented, 'it would be quite impossible to fly the machine.'

Superintendent George Reed, head of the Hitchin Police division, confirmed that a large piece of the engine bonnet was found three hundred yards from the crash point, adding that it was almost certainly this big object falling through the air just prior to the crash dive which led some witnesses to assume mistakenly that one of the airmen had fallen out. Major Brooke Popham

The Daily Mirror

THE MORNING JOURNAL WITH THE SECOND LARGEST NET SALE.

No. 2,773.   THURSDAY, SEPTEMBER 12, 1912   One Halfpenny.

THE SERVICES' TRIBUTE TO TWO HEROIC ARMY AIRMEN: IMPRESSIVE SCENES AT THE FUNERAL OF CAPTAIN HAMILTON AND LIEUTENANT WYNESS-STUART.

Crowds lined the streets of Hitchin yesterday, when the bodies of Captain Hamilton and Lieutenant Wyness-Stuart, the two Army officers who lost their lives in Friday's aeroplane disaster, were removed from the mortuary to the railway-station for conveyance to their respective burial places at Hythe, Kent, and Wells, Somerset. At Oxford the inquest was held on Second-Lieutenant Hotchkiss and Lieutenant Bettington, the two officers who also laid down their lives in the execution of their duty. (1) Officers of the Naval Flying School saluting as the coffins pass by. (2) The gun-carriages on which the coffins were placed. That bearing the remains of Captain Hamilton is seen in the foreground. They were followed by a military escort, which included Regulars, Yeomanry and Territorials. The portraits are of Captain Hamilton, who is wearing an airman's hat, and Lieutenant Wyness-Stuart.—(Daily Mirror and C.N.)

There was similar national news coverage of the hero's funeral accorded the two dead aviators at Hitchin.

114

revealed the irony that the aeroplane in which the two officers died had, only a few weeks earlier, won a £2,000 prize when flown by a Frenchman during the trials and competitions on Salisbury Plain. Captain Hamilton, he said, had flown this machine for only three hours, but was used to similar machines. The jury returned a verdict of accidental death and paid tribute to the valour of the aviators. Patrick Hamilton and Atholl Wyness-Stuart were the first servicemen to die in a military aircraft while flying under military orders – the first fliers to die on active service. The deaths were sadly the prelude to a number of disasters which clouded the first year of the Royal Flying Corps. A week later, two more colleagues taking part in the manoeuvres. Lieutenant E. H. Hotchkiss and Lieutenant C. A. Bettington, died in a similar crash near Oxford.

It was, however, the Graveley air disaster which brought home to the public with brutal suddenness the fact that the young men pioneering military aviation were engaged in an occupation that contained far more danger than glamour. Inevitably Hamilton and Wyness-Stuart, who were both aged 30, were accorded a hero's funeral. Hundreds of townspeople and villagers turned up for the service at St Saviour's Church, but since it was completely filled by family mourners and members of the Armed Services, they could only stand outside in silence, hoping to catch a few words of the eloquent tributes and the hymn that had been composed especially for the event:

'Direct with thine all-seeing eye
Watch each dread journey through the sky;
Through every storm and danger zone,
Bring each brave pilot safely home.'

The airmen's coffins, borne by comrades of the Royal Flying Corps, were carried out to the gun-carriages; a military band, playing a funeral lament, led the cortege to Hitchin railway station past crowds lining the road ten deep in places. From Hitchin, the coffins were taken to different parts of England for private burial – Captain Hamilton's, at his mother's request, to Hythe in Kent, Lieutenant Wyness-Stuart's, accompanied by his young widow, to Wells in Somerset. That week in Hitchin a memorial

115

IN MEMORY OF
CAPTAIN HAMILTON,
AND
LIEU: WYNESS STUART,
OF THE ROYAL FLYING CORPS
WHO LOST THEIR LIVES WHILST
SERVING THEIR COUNTRY
AS AVIATORS. SEP 6TH 1912.

ERECTED BY LOCAL SUBSCRIPTION

The memorial which still stands on the roadside between Wymondley and Willian, close to the field where the airmen died.

fund was opened and a stone-mason put to work, and in the last week of September a large crowd gathered once again near the field where the Deperdussin had crashed. The small granite obelisk, bearing the names of the aviators, was erected – not in the meadow where they had died – but half a mile away by the side of the road that runs between Willian and Wymondley. Captain Hamilton's mother laid a wreath of chrysanthemums upon it and his flight commander made a short speech.

'Some people,' said Major Brooke Popham, 'may think a memorial stone a waste of money and that it would have been more profitable to give it to the hospital or some local charity. I beg to differ. We should be a poor nation without recollections of noble deeds and heroic deaths to inspire us. The careless child and the weary wayfarer will pass along this road, look at this stone, read this inscription and realise that they, too, have a duty to perform. They will know that patriotism it not an empty word and that Englishmen are still ready to lay down their lives in the service of their country.'

Two years later, events in Europe proved only too well how right the major was.

116

Death from the Sky

★

The county town of Hertford was a sitting duck the night the Zeppelins attacked. In 1915, despite persistent warnings from the War Office about the new danger of aerial bombardment, most of the country still did not understand the horrors involved. So when local councils were urged to impose night-time blackouts in the more heavily populated areas of Eastern England, not everyone took the warning seriously. In Hertford's case the authorities made a gesture by reducing the intensity of the street lighting but there was no effort at all to persuade householders or shopkeepers to darken their premises. As a result, on the night of October 13, when five German Zeppelins crossed the North Sea on a mission to bomb London, Hertford was 'ablaze with illumination' and, because of that, its townspeople were among the first to experience that particularly evil development in 20th century warfare – the indiscriminate bombing of civilians.

There was much talk of the war in the town that night. The county newspaper the *Hertfordshire Mercury* was publishing casualty lists each week, along with more cheering but well-censored reports of how the local regiments were faring in France. Nowhere was the situation under more intense scrutiny than at Lombard House, headquarters of the local Conservative Association, in Bull Plain. Many of Hertford's older professional and businessmen were there that night; doctors, a dentist, shopkeepers, millers and council officials among them.

At 8.40 p.m. the conversation was interrupted by the steady throbbing of engines. Someone ran in to tell them that a Zeppelin was approaching whereupon, instead of dimming the lights and taking cover, almost the entire club membership emptied out into the garden to watch the enemy airship's progress over the town. This one was, apparently, after bigger game for it ploughed on steadily southwards towards London. More than 500 feet

A German Schutte-Lanz Airship in its hangar.

long (half as long again as a football pitch) and 90 feet high, it was undoubtedly an awe-inspiring sight in the night sky. A gigantic silver-grey cigar, capable of speeds of 55 miles an hour, carrying a crew of 20 and armed with machine guns and up to five tons of high explosive bombs. With something new to talk about the club members returned inside to continue drinking and debating. A little more than an hour later, another Zeppelin, the L16, appeared to the east of the town. Once more, glass in hand, members strolled out onto the lawns to witness the passing of the second visitor. Much of the rest of the town was watching, too.

'This time,' a reporter on the *Mercury* wrote later, 'the Zeppelin shut off its engines and came down to a much lower altitude. It floated across the town in a rapid glide as the clocks were striking ten. As it released its cargo of death-dealing bombs the effect was stupefying.'

In less than two minutes the crew of the Zeppelin dropped 44 bombs on Hertford – 30 incendiary and 14 high explosive – cutting

Some of the German crew who perished in the SL 11 over Cuffley. The Commander, Wilhelm Schramm, is on the right.

a swathe of damage across the heart of the town, beginning in The Meads and traversing Hartham, The Folly, Bull Plain, The Wash, Mill Bridge and Old Cross, before it ended with two explosions in the grounds of the hospital. In that two minutes, nine lives were lost, 15 people were wounded, ten buildings completely destroyed and more than 100 damaged. Bull Plain and The Conservative Club got the worst of it. Four prominent townsmen were killed outright as they stood in the grounds still not appreciating the danger they were in. As the gruesome evidence at the inquest revealed, Hertford's Borough Surveyor John Jevons, aged 57, was literally blown to pieces; James Gregory, aged 55, a music teacher and organist at All Saint's Church, also died from multiple injuries, as did a local draper George Cartledge, aged 56 and Ernest Jolly, 27, one of the staff at the Hertford branch of Barclays Bank. Further up the street a workman Mr Charlie Spicer was caught in the blast and killed. At Number 37 Bull Plain, George Game, aged four, was asleep in bed with his elder brother. Their room caught the full force of the flying masonry from that same bomb. Little George died later from head injuries – his brother escaped unhurt.

Further across town two workers at Garratt's Flour Mill were killed when caught by the blast of another high explosive bomb, and an off-duty soldier died after being hit by shrapnel as he walked his girlfriend home. At Holt's Mill, incendiary bombs caused a fire which destroyed half the building, killing most of the mill's horses which were trapped inside. 'Considering the densely-populated area,' wrote the *Mercury's* reporter, 'it is a wonder more were not killed. The effect of terror on the civilians was remarkable. Many who were safe indoors ran out terrified, unconsciously placing themselves in greater danger, while many others who were outdoors flung themselves flat on the pavements. Others fell to their knees calling on God to save them. The Zeppelin, having finished its foul work, made a majestic sweep round and momentarily hovered above the town as if to see the effect of its handiwork – the pirates on board no doubt expecting some big conflagrations – and, pointing its nose north-eastwards, disappeared in the clouds.'

In fact, the newspaper's account of the Zeppelin raid didn't appear until more than three years after the event. So strict was the war-time press censorship that, at the time, the *Mercury* was not even allowed to mention its own town – only that 'a fleet of hostile airships had visited the Eastern Counties and a portion of the London area.' However, the sparse ten-line statement did confirm that during the various attacks that night 71 people had been killed and another 128 injured. It was the German airships' most damaging raid of the war.

At the inquest on Hertford's nine bomb victims the jury urged the council to enforce much stricter blackout precautions. Endorsing their comment the Coroner Mr Phillip Longmore added: 'We all view this horrible thing with great revulsion and we cannot but have the greatest hatred for those who brought it about.... I am perfectly certain that such monstrous deeds will have to be punished in some other way. It will make us Englishmen all the more determined to see this war through and ensure that the perpetration of these horrors on defenceless citizens is punished.'

In fact, that same airship, the L16, returned to make further bombing raids and to kill more Hertfordshire people. Yet, revenge against the Zeppelin fleet was due to take place in spectacular fashion the following year – and only a few miles from Hertford. It was an event that would also mark the beginning of the end of the airship raids against England.

At the time of the raid on Hertford in 1915, Zeppelins and similar German airships were considered to be impregnable. They could operate at a height of 12,000 feet, often out of range of the anti-aircraft guns and searchlights and too high for the handful of outdated Royal Flying Corps aircraft that were sent up to seek them out. However, during the following year an important 'secret weapon' was perfected which was to turn the tables on the German invaders. This was an incendiary bullet, which contained a mixture of explosive and phosphorus and which could puncture the gigantic envelope of an airship, enter the gas cells and ignite the highly volatile hydrogen gas which until the introduction of the safer helium, was the only lighter-than-air gas that could be used in airships. By the summer of 1916 the Brock-Pomeroy incendiaries were tested and issued to the RFC Home Defence Squadrons – just in time to confront what the Germans *hoped* would be the biggest and most devastating airship raid England had known.

On the evening of Saturday, September 2nd, an armada of 16 Zeppelins and Schutte-Lanz airships, the combined fleets of the German Army and Navy, set off across the North Sea with a total load of more than 500 bombs in their racks. Of the 16, two developed engine trouble and had to return, but the remainder crossed the coast at 10.40 p.m., some heading for Lincolnshire and Nottinghamshire, the majority bearing south on London. By 10.30 p.m. they had reached Hertfordshire – the infamous L16 among them. This time 'the child-killers' as they had become known, released a clutch of bombs on the village of Essendon, severely damaging the church of St Mary the Virgin. Terrified by the noise of the explosions 12 year old Eleanor Bamford, daughter of the village blacksmith, dashed out of her cottage in panic. Her elder sister Frances, aged 26, ran after her to comfort her. Both were cut down by flying shrapnel from one of the

121

Leefe Robinson with the BE2C biplane in which he shot down the airship
– a souvenir fragment of which is displayed by his ground crew.

L16's bombs; Frances was killed immediately, her young sister
died in hospital the following day.

Later that night over North London a Schutte-Lanz airship,
the SL11, was scattering bombs fairly ineffectively over Finsbury
Park, Tottenham and Enfield. RFC pilot Lt William Leefe Robinson, on patrol from his airfield at Suttons Farm, Hornchurch,
spotted the invader trapped in the beams of searchlights and
dodging shell-bursts. The 21 year old aviator had been on patrol
in his frail BE2c bi-plane for three hours and was running low
on fuel. He went into a dive to gain on the airship and, ignoring
the dangerous possibility that he could be shot down by the shells
of his fellow countrymen, he flew up under the gigantic monster
and – with his solitary Lewis gun – emptied an entire drum of
ammunition into its belly. It seemed to have no effect. By this
time the crew of the airship were firing at him as well but this
didn't deter Leefe Robinson from banking round to distribute
yet another drum of incendiaries this time into the SL11's side
– but again without apparent effect. 'I then got behind it,' the
young officer wrote later in his log. 'By this time I was very close
– 500 feet or less below and concentrated one drum on one part

Lieutenant William Leefe Robinson VC.

(underneath rear). I was then at a height of 11,500 feet... I had hardly finished the drum before I saw the part fired at glow. In a few seconds the whole rear part was blazing... I quickly got out of the way of the falling blazing Zeppelin (sic) and being very excited fired off a few red Very's lights and dropped a parachute flare. Having very little oil and petrol left I returned to Sutton's Farm, landing at 2.45 a.m.'

123

A postcard memento of the last moments of the SL 11.

The fiery destruction of the SL11 was witnessed by thousands of jubilant people on the ground and it has been said that no single incident during the First World War created a greater sensation. For months the airships had killed and maimed innocent civilians, apparently with impunity, and the knowledge that one had at last been destroyed provided a much-needed boost to British morale.

The wooden-framed airship fell into a field behind *The Plough Inn* at Cuffley, where it burned furiously for more than two hours. The crew, of course, were all killed but fortunately no civilians were hurt. So big was the explosion that it could be seen forty miles away and consequently was witnessed by the crews of all the other airships, who decided to turn tail and head for the coast, dropping their remaining bombs as they fled. There was no censorship on this story – which dominated the front page of every newspaper for weeks to come. At daylight, the little-known village of Cuffley was besieged by sightseers and souvenir hunters. 60,000 came by car, train, pony and trap or on foot. The roads became blocked, the pub ran out of food and drink and a violent cloudburst added to the chaos, turning the field into a quagmire. Somewhat diffidently the boyish victor Lt Leefe Robinson arrived during the afternoon to view his handiwork and was immediately mobbed by cheering troops who had been busy clearing the wreckage. They presented him with several souvenirs including an Iron Cross, a revolver and the scorched log of the airship. As a national hero it was only a matter of days before the aviator was summoned to Windsor Castle where King George V awarded him The Victoria Cross 'for most conspicuous bravery.' It was the first VC to be won in action over British soil.

For many people, though, the whole euphoria of the airship's destruction was soured by a tactless War Office decision to give the 16 dead airmen from the SL11 a military funeral in Potters Bar on the very day that two victims of the bombing, the Bamford sisters, were being buried at the adjoining village of Essendon. Letters of protest flooded in and the Vicar of Potters Bar was threatened with a riot if he gave 'the German murderers' a Christian burial. However, apart from one woman throwing some eggs at the cortege as it went by, the event itself passed off with

Soldiers dismantling the remains of the burnt-out airship engine.

dignity. Even so, there were many who shared the views expressed by the editor of the *Barnet Press* in a vitriolic leading article published the following Saturday: 'So, we buried with military honours the baked Huns brought down at Cuffley. Military honours for murderers and a Christian burial service. What hypocrisy!... We have seen a village church and vicarage wrecked by Zeppelin bombs, cottages razed to the ground, amongst the ruins of which was found the body of a poor woman while a girl, still living, but with a leg torn off, was rescued in agony that ended in death.'

Within a month two more airships were shot down by the Royal Flying Corps patrols, one over Great Burstead in Essex and another close to Cuffley – at Oakmere Farm, Potters Bar. In all ten were destroyed during the war, and more than 200 German airship crew killed. But it was that first loss – the SL11 – which marked the end of the Zeppelin offensive against Britain. The Germans re-designed the ships to enable them to reach great-

Another popular postcard, thousands of which were sold in the weeks after the airship was shot down.

er heights but this was not successful and the decreased accuracy of their bombing and navigation, coupled with the problems caused by oxygen deficiency, meant they were no longer able to maintain supremacy against the improved flying machines and aerial weaponry developed by Britain.

After being taken by the War Office on a morale-boosting tour of the country, during which he was showered with gifts worth several thousand pounds, Lt William Leefe Robinson VC returned to active duty as a Captain and Flight Commander. He was posted to France and captured by the Germans after his aircraft suffered engine failure and crash-landed behind enemy lines. He made several unsuccessful attempts to escape and because of this was eventually placed in solitary confinement, where he remained until the Armistice was signed in 1918. He arrived home at Stanmore in Middlesex, on December 14th in a very weak condition caused, said his family, by the appalling treatment he received while a prisoner of war. Over Christmas he fell victim to the severe influenza epidemic that was sweeping the country and on the last day of the year, he died. He was 23. However, his courageous exploits are not forgotten. A short distance from the churchyard of All Saint's Stanmore, where he lies, there is *The Leefe Robinson* public house which proudly displays a host of mementoes of 'The Victor of Cuffley'; while at Cuffley itself there is a monument erected at the end of the war by readers of the *The Daily Express*. This was restored recently, so ensuring that future generations learn of the deeds of the handsome young aviator who took on a giant and gave England a hero just when it needed one.